New York Observed

JAMES E. ALLEN

VERNON HOWE BAILEY

New York Observed

Artists and Writers Look at the City, 1650 to the Present

Compiled and Edited by Barbara Cohen, Seymour Chwast, and Steven Heller

Introduction by Kate Simon

Harry N. Abrams, Inc., Publishers, New York

Acknowledgments

The editors would like to give very special thanks to Margaret Donovan, our editor at Abrams, without whose intelligence and caring this book would have been impossible to complete.

The following were also extremely important to this project: Lita Talarico, Sam Antupit, Sarah Jane Freymann, Kevin Gatta, Roxanne Slimak, Abby Fells, Edward Spiro, Peter Cohen, Lee Cohen, Myron Cohen, Barbara Voorsanger (Urban Graphics), Mary Ryan (Mary Ryan Gallery), Harry Orth (Department of English, the University of Vermont), and Barbara and Gilbert Millstein.

And special appreciation to Joseph Mitchell.

For Pushpin Editions:

Producer: Steven Heller
Designer: Seymour Chwast
Associate Designer: Kevin Gatta
Production: Roxanne Slimak
Research: Lita Talarico

For Harry N. Abrams, Inc.:

Editor: Margaret Donovan
Art Director: Samuel N. Antupit

Library of Congress Cataloging-in-Publication Data

New York observed.

   Includes indexes.
   1. Arts, American. 2. New York (N.Y.) in art.
I. Cohen, Barbara (Barbara L.) II. Chwast, Seymour.
III. Heller, Steven.
NX503.N5 1987 700'.973   86–22134
ISBN 0–8109–2343–2 (pbk.)

Times Mirror Books

Printed and bound in Japan

Contents

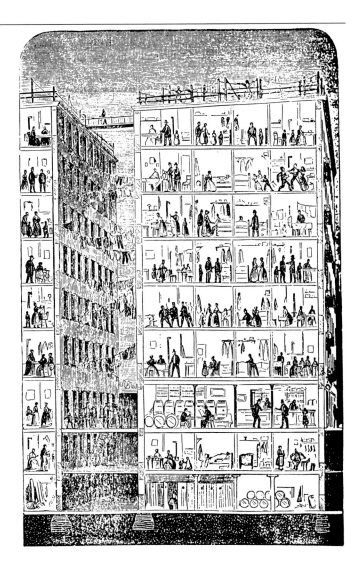

ISAC FRIEDLANDER

Introduction

I am constantly astonished at the oceans of words a young city like New York spills concerning itself, a good sampling of that spill collected in the pages that follow. We haven't, of course, the accumulations of Rome or Paris or London and certainly not the ancient voices of Jerusalem, yet we seem to have gathered spates of prosody in a splendid variety. It soars in the hyperbolic cadences of Thomas Wolfe's description of the city's "wonderful, secret thrill of some impending ecstasy" and Walt Whitman's full-throated hymns, settles down to the keen, affectionate portraits by Joseph Mitchell, and sinks to mutterings of complaint—by Mark Twain, for one. What produces it all? Considerable vanity and the quality Joyce Kilmer describes here as our "delight in the whimsical, the inconsistent, the unexpected."

Poking its way through these words and pictures that vaunt, as Dreiser puts it, the "power, energy, strength, life, beauty, terror" is a telling paradox. The energy and restless change it bespeaks are themselves immutable characteristics of the city as well as the pauses that stop for repetitions, for echoes. As a friend complains of rising rents, we hear behind his words Philip Hone's voice carrying similar lamentation in 1835. Sitting on a Fifth Avenue bus, becoming imbedded, like a fly in glue, in imprisoning traffic makes us the inheritors of carriages mired in the traffic of lower Broadway when that was a main thoroughfare. Cockroaches here, there, everywhere are diminutive present-day versions of the pigs that once roamed the streets as our only sanitation department. New York was a city of bicycles in Stephen Crane's day; we are suffering a much less chic, a much rougher, revival. And so on and so on and so on.

One constant wonderment is the adjustability of the rushing, impatient, stereotypical New Yorker, his tolerance of the excesses of his city and his forgiving pleasure in its atonements. We permit, for instance, our sky to be obliterated by skyscrapers biting off each other's eccentric heads and forgive them by strolling in the gentle mood of Chinese poets among their flowers and appealing, foolish little waters. My neighborhood, Kips Bay and its environs, has afforded me absorbing study in my own adjustability. Crossing Park Avenue South, I must admire the courage of me and my neighbors in the games of traffic mayhem. Traduced by the lying WALK signals, we are trapped between the curving path of a taxi Juggernaut and a bicycle whose rider has the arrogant scorn of a mounted Crusader having at the pagans in his path. My section of Lexington Avenue which once upon a time (a decade or two here takes on the patina of myth) held a cluster of Middle Eastern restaurants is now solidly and repetitiously East Indian, with four restaurants on one block and sari, ghee, and chutney shops piled on each other. This may be a prosaic example of Delmore Schwartz's

"It is the city consciousness/Which sees and says: more: more and more: always more." So, if I can't get humus as a starter for my dinner, I'll begin by munching on chapati.

Our neighborhood sports prostitutes in red pants tight enough to be paint. I decide—adjust?—that they are welcome guardians for my night sauntering. The Bosch canvas of blank-faced people, the shouters of obscenities into the indifferent air, shades of generations of New York derelicts, insist, by their very number, that I become accustomed to them and I do. Like most seasoned New Yorkers I walk wary but not afraid and, in the constant exploration of the wonders of any street, find myself admiring the devoted drinking couple, decorated with paperbound bottles, contentedly slouching in the afternoon shade of a tree. And I wonder where they are now, the printers of the purple footsteps on my sidewalks. My neighborhood evenings give me, as well, the jeweled cap on the Chrysler Building, the colorful moods of the Empire State Building, and far to the west, a bright pink sash of sky that is my sunset.

The city also feeds me a nice nostalgia, a gentle deploring, never mournful. Surrounded by the beamish South Street Seaport complex, I find myself looking for the crazy bazaar that was the Eagle Bag and Burlap Company, now buried somewhere under the optimistic commonplace, and for the full slosh and shine of the Fulton Fish Market before its dwindling. For our collective, tribal nostalgia I look at the old pictures in museums and leaf through books like this one, hoping they will restore for me the ships, the stevedores, the wagons and dray horses that arrowed into the city on the waters of Coenties Slip, now dry, gray, and stilled. There is consolation, though, in heading southward to South Ferry and gazing back at the architectural tonalities and textures that create a remarkable tapestry.

Most of us rather enjoy, too, the loud overaccenting, the phoniness that tried to lure Europeans to these shores with engravings of stately palm trees brushing our waters. That same mildly crooked quality sits on Columbus Avenue, not too long ago listless and shabby, now assuming the classy airs of the Champs-Elysées. It taints the shops of our alchemists, who try to present dross as gold and our restaurants, which offer essentially Oliver Twist fare at Lucullan prices, but I don't somehow mind too much: amused, adjusted. As E. B. White has it in *Here Is New York*, after a jeremiad about living here being unworkable, "implausible": "But the city makes up for its hazards and its deficiencies by supplying its citizens with massive doses of a supplementary vitamin—the sense of belonging to something unique, cosmopolitan, mighty and unparalleled."

—Kate Simon

MAXFIELD PARRISH

Truman Capote

The Diamond Iceberg

1950

It is a myth, the city, the rooms and windows, the steam-spitting streets; for anyone, everyone, a different myth, an idol-head with traffic-light eyes winking a tender green, a cynical red. This island, floating in river water like a diamond iceberg, call it New York, name it whatever you like; the name hardly matters because, entering from the greater reality of elsewhere, one is only in search of a city, a place to hide, to lose or discover oneself, to make a dream wherein you prove that perhaps after all you are not an ugly duckling, but wonderful, and worthy of love, as you thought sitting on the stoop where the Fords went by; as you thought planning your search for a city. . . .

Washington Irving

Golden Dreams

from *Tales of a Traveller*
1824

Wolfert Webber went to bed with a heavy heart; and it was long before the golden visions that disturbed his brain, permitted him to sink into repose. The same visions, however, extended into his sleeping thoughts, and assumed a more definite form. He dreamt that he had discovered an immense treasure in the centre of his garden. At every stroke of the spade he laid bare a golden ingot; diamond crosses sparkled out of the dust; bags of money turned up their bellies, corpulent with pieces of eight, or venerable doubloons; and chests, wedged close with moidores, ducats, and pistareens, yawned before his ravished eyes, and vomited forth their glittering contents.

Wolfert awoke a poorer man than ever. He had no heart to go about his daily concerns, which appeared so paltry and profitless; but sat all day long in the chimney-corner, picturing to himself ingots and heaps of gold in the fire. The next night his dream was repeated. He was again in his garden, digging, and laying open stores of hidden wealth. There was something very singular in this repetition. He passed another day of reverie, and though it was cleaning-day, and the house, as usual in Dutch households, completely topsy-turvy, yet he sat unmoved amidst the general uproar.

The third night he went to bed with a palpitating heart. He put on his red nightcap, wrong side outwards for good luck. It was deep midnight before his anxious mind could settle itself into sleep. Again the golden dream was repeated, and again he saw his garden teeming with ingots and money-bags.

Wolfert rose the next morning in complete bewilderment. A dream three times repeated was never known to lie; and if so, his fortune was made. . . .

His grand care now was how to secure this immense treasure without it being known. Instead of working regularly in his grounds in the daytime, he now stole from his bed at night, and with spade and pickaxe, went to work to rip up and dig about his paternal acres, from one end to the other. In a little time the whole garden, which had presented such a goodly and regular appearance, with its phalanx of cabbages, like a vegetable army in battle array, was reduced to a scene of devastation, while the relentless Wolfert, with nightcap on head, and lantern and spade in hand, stalked through the slaughtered ranks, the destroying angel of his own vegetable world. . . .

In the meantime the seasons gradually rolled on. The little frogs that had piped in the meadows in early spring, croaked as bullfrogs in the brooks during the summer heats, and then sunk into silence. The peach tree budded, blossomed, and bore its fruit. The swallows and martins came, twittered about the roof, built their nests, reared their young, held their congress along the eaves, and then winged their flight in search of another spring. The caterpillar spun its winding-sheet, dangled in it from the great buttonwood tree that shaded the house, turned into a moth, fluttered with the last sunshine of summer, and disappeared; and finally the leaves of the buttonwood tree turned yellow, then brown, then rustled one by one to the ground, and whirling about in little eddies of wind and dust, whispered that winter was at hand.

Wolfert gradually awoke from his dream of wealth as the year declined. He had reared no crop to supply the wants of his household during the sterility of winter. The season was long and severe, and for the first time the family was really straightened in its comforts. By degrees a revulsion of thought took place in Wolfert's mind, common to those whose golden dreams have been disturbed by pinching realities. . . .

Haggard care gathered about his brow; he went about with a money-seeking air, his eyes bent downwards into the dust, and carrying his hands in his pockets, as men are apt to do when they have nothing else to put into them. He could not even pass the city almshouse without giving it a rueful glance, as if destined to be his future abode.

The strangeness of his conduct and of his looks occasioned much speculation and remark. For a long time he was suspected of being crazy, and then everybody pitied him; at length it began to be suspected that he was poor, and then everybody avoided him. . . .

Dirk Waldron was the only being that seemed to shed a ray of sunshine into this house of mourning. He came in with cheery look and manly spirit, and tried to reanimate the expiring heart of the poor money-digger, but it was all in vain. Wolfert was completely done over. If any thing was wanting to complete his despair, it was a notice served upon him in the midst of his distress, that the corporation were about to run a new street through the very centre of his cabbage garden. He saw nothing before him but poverty and ruin; his last reliance, the garden of his forefathers, was to be laid waste, and what then was to become of his poor wife and child?...

The lawyer was brought—a dapper, bustling, round-headed little man, Roorback (or Rollebuck, as it was pronounced) by name. At the sight of him the women broke into loud lamentations, for they looked upon the signing of a will as the signing of a death-warrant. Wolfert made a feeble motion for them to be silent. Poor Amy buried her face and her grief in the bed-curtain. Dame Webber resumed her knitting to hide her distress, which betrayed itself, however, in a pellucid tear, that trickled silently down and hung at the end of her peaked nose; while the cat, the only unconcerned member of the family, played with the good dame's ball of worsted, as it rolled about the floor.

Wolfert lay on his back, his nightcap drawn over his forehead; his eyes closed; his whole visage the picture of death. He begged the lawyer to be brief, for he felt his end approaching, and that he had no time to lose. The lawyer nibbed his pen, spread out his paper, and prepared to write.

"I give and bequeath," said Wolfert, faintly, "my small farm—"

"What—all!" exclaimed the lawyer.

Wolfert half opened his eyes and looked upon the lawyer.

"Yes—all," said he.

"What! all that great patch of land with cabbages and sunflowers, which the corporation is just going to run a main street through?"

"The same," said Wolfert, with a heavy sigh and sinking back upon his pillow.

"I wish him joy that inherits it!" said the little lawyer, chuckling and rubbing his hands involuntarily.

"What do you mean?" said Wolfert, again opening his eyes.

"That he'll be one of the richest men in the place!" cried little Rollebuck.

THOMAS NAST

The expiring Wolfert seemed to step back from the threshold of existence: his eyes again lighted up; he raised himself in his bed, shoved back his red worsted nightcap, and stared broadly at the lawyer.

"You don't say so!" exclaimed he.

"Faith, but I do!" rejoined the other. "Why, when that great field and that piece of meadow come to be laid out in streets, and cut up into snug building lots—why, whoever owns them need not pull off his hat to the patroon!"

"Say you so?" cried Wolfert, half thrusting one leg out of bed, "why, then I think I'll not make my will yet!"

To the surprise of everybody the dying man actually recovered. The vital spark which had glimmered faintly in the socket, received fresh fuel from the oil of gladness, which the little lawyer poured into his soul. It once more burnt up into a flame.

Give physic to the heart, ye who would revive the body of a spirit-broken man! In a few days Wolfert left his room; in a few days more his table was covered with deeds, plans of streets and building lots. Little Rollebuck was constantly with him, his right-hand man and adviser, and instead of making his will, assisted in the more agreeable task of making his fortune. In fact, Wolfert Webber was one of those worthy Dutch burghers of the Manhattoes whose fortunes have been made, in a manner, in spite of themselves; who have tenaciously held on to their hereditary acres, raising turnips and cabbages about the skirts of the city, hardly able to make both ends meet, until the corporation has cruelly driven streets through their abodes, and they have suddenly awakened out of a lethargy, and, to their astonishment, found themselves rich men.

Before many months had elapsed a great bustling street passed through the very centre of the Webber garden, just where Wolfert had dreamed of finding a treasure. His golden dream was accomplished; he did indeed find an unlooked-for source of wealth; for, when his paternal lands were distributed into building lots, and rented out to safe tenants, instead of producing a paltry crop of cabbages, they returned him an abundant crop of rents; insomuch that on quarter day it was a goodly sight to see his tenants rapping at his door, from morning to night, each with a little round-bellied bag of money, the golden produce of the soil.

Mark Helprin

A Winter's Tale
1983

Manhattan, a high narrow kingdom as hopeful as any that ever was, burst upon him full force, a great and imperfect steel-tressed palace of a hundred million chambers, many-tiered gardens, pools, passages, and ramparts above its rivers. Built upon an island from which bridges stretched to other islands and to the mainland, the palace of a thousand tall towers was undefended. It took in nearly all who wished to enter, being so much larger than anything else that it could not ever be conquered but only visited by force. Newcomers, invaders, and the inhabitants themselves were so confused by its multiplicity, variety, vanity, size, brutality, and grace, that they lost sight of what it was. It was, for sure, one simple structure, busily divided, lovely and pleasing, an extraordinary hive of the imagination, the greatest house ever built.

Marie Ganz and Nat Ferber
Rebels
1920

But however disconnected and far apart the few scenes that still come back to me from the first years of my life, I have glimpses of our arrival in New York that are as vivid as if it had been only yesterday. In a quiet hour alone I wave the years away, and I am a child again, trudging along beside my father, who, weighted down with the great rolls of bedding we had brought with us from the old home, is guiding us through strange, noisy streets. I am staring in wonder at the great buildings and the never-ending crowds of people. I am frightened, bewildered, ready to cry. I keep a tiny hand twisted in the tail of my father's coat, fearing to lose him.

At last we turn into a dark, dirty alley, which runs like a tunnel under a tenement house and leads us to our future home in the building in the rear.

Oh, how hot and stuffy were those two little rooms that we entered! The city was scorching under one of the hot waves that bring such untold misery to the tenements. Not a breath of air stirred. The place was an oven. But, flushed with heat and perspiring though he was, my father ushered us in with a great show of joy and enthusiasm. Suddenly his smile gave way to an expression that reflected bitter disappointment and injured pride as he became aware of the disgust which my mother could not conceal.

"So we have crossed half the world for this!" she cried, thinking bitterly of the comfortable farmhouse we had left behind us.

* * *

An errand girl was wanted by a modiste in Fifth Avenue. A job on Fifth Avenue, the street of the rich! My imagination began to stir. What tales I had heard of that street—of its splendid homes, its great hotels, its stores where one could spend a fortune on a bit of jewelry, on a tiny vase that the squeeze of a rough hand might shatter into dust, on a dress that might be spoiled in a night; what tales of its endless procession of carriages and automobiles, its myriads of sparkling electric lights that turned the darkness into day! Of course I had never been there, unless possibly I had caught a glimpse of it on that wonderful ride I had taken with the stranger when I was a small child. We children of the ghetto's poor never, unless through some miracle, strayed so far from our own neighbourhood as that. Indeed very few of the grown folks among us ever went beyond the bounds of the lower East Side. Riding in street cars was expensive, and nickels were too scarce to be squandered on such extravagance as sight-seeing. So it was little we really knew of the strange world that lay just beyond our own domain—of the region that lay before us dim and mysterious in the distance on summer nights as we stood on the house-tops.

"You think I could find Fifth Avenue, Ichael?" I asked doubtfully.

"Sure," he answered. "You keep walking up the Bowery and asking the policemens. It ain't hard finding the way anywhere if you keep asking the policemens."

"Give me the piece out of the paper," I said. "I'm going."

And so it was that I went out that morning into the undiscovered country. A thrilling journey it was through all those unknown streets, and when I came to the great avenue that was my goal I was dazed with its wonders. Crowds I was accustomed to, for the ghetto's streets were always swarming with people, but not with such people as I saw now. How tall the men and women were! How strange their faces! What wonderful clothes they wore! How motionless they held themselves as they talked—no gesturing of hands, no shrugging of shoulders. Truly I had discovered a new race of human beings.

I came at last, as if walking in a dream, to the shop whose advertisement I carried in my hand. It was a very fine shop with great silken curtains in the windows and trees growing in pots at the doorway. But inside it was even more impressive, not only because of its rich furnishings but because of the glory that seemed to be reflected all over it from the magnificence of the woman who was its boss. Many a dressmaker I had seen, but never one that bore the faintest resemblance to the woman who ran that shop. Here was a dressmaker who wore the clothes of a queen, or at any rate such clothes as I imagined queens must wear, and who carried herself with truly royal dignity; a dressmaker whose clean, polished, carefully-trimmed fingernails bore no traces of the toil of her trade, whose hands were white and soft, even to the tips of the fingers, with not one callous spot, not one sign of a needle prick. She was tall and stout and had a mass of vivid red hair. Her eyes were as grey, cold and unwavering as an eagle's. Never before had I met a woman of such majestic appearance. Indeed she was the first woman I had ever spoken with in my life who was not of the ghetto.

Michael Gold

Jews Without Money

1930

The East Side of New York was then the city's red light district, a vast 606 playground under the business management of Tammany Hall. The Jews had fled from the European pogroms; with prayer, thanksgiving and solemn faith from a new Egypt into a New Promised Land.

They found awaiting them the sweatshops, the bawdy houses and Tammany Hall.

There were hundreds of prostitutes on my street. They occupied vacant stores, they crowded into flats and apartments in all the tenements. The pious Jews hated the traffic. But they were pauper strangers here; they could do nothing. They shrugged their shoulders, and murmured: "This is America." They tried to live.

They tried to shut their eyes. We children did not shut our eyes. We saw and knew.

On sunshiny days the whores sat on chairs along the sidewalks. They sprawled indolently, their legs taking up half the pavements. People stumbled over a gauntlet of whores' meaty legs.

The girls gossiped and chirped like a jungle of parrots. Some knitted shawls and stockings. Others hummed. Others chewed Russian sunflower seeds and monotonously spat out the shells.

The girls winked and jeered, made lascivious gestures at passing males. They pulled at coat-tails and cajoled men with fake honeyed words. They called their wares like pushcart peddlers. At five years I knew what it was they sold.

O. Henry

The Sparrows in Madison Square

from *Waifs and Strays*
1917

The young man in straitened circumstances who comes to New York City to enter literature has but one thing to do, provided he has studied carefully his field in advance. He must go straight to Madison Square, write an article about the sparrows there, and sell it to the *Sun* for $15.

I cannot recall either a novel or a story dealing with the popular theme of the young writer from the provinces who comes to the metropolis to win fame and fortune with his pen in which the boy does not get his start that way. It does seem strange that some author, in casting about for startlingly original plots, has not hit upon the idea of having his hero write about the bluebirds in Union Square and sell it to the *Herald*. But a search through the files of metropolitan fiction counts up overwhelmingly for the sparrows and the old Garden Square, and the *Sun* always writes the check.

Of course it is easy to understand why this first city venture of the budding author is always successful. He is primed by necessity to a superlative effort; mid the iron and stone and marble of the roaring city he has found this spot of singing birds and green grass and trees; every tender sentiment in his nature is battling with the sweet pain of homesickness; his genius is aroused as it never may be again; the birds chirp, the tree branches sway, the noise of wheels is forgotten; he writes with his soul in his pen—and sells it to the *Sun* for $15.

I had read of this custom during many years before I came to New York. When my friends were using their strongest arguments to dissuade me from coming, I only smiled serenely. They did not know of that sparrow graft I had up my sleeve.

When I arrived in New York, and the car took me straight from the ferry up Twenty-third Street to Madison Square, I could hear that $15 check rustling in my inside pocket.

I obtained lodging at an unhyphenated hostelry, and the next morning I was on a bench in Madison Square almost by the time the sparrows were awake. Their melodious chirping, the benignant spring foliage of the noble trees and the clean, fragrant grass reminded me so potently of the old farm I had left that tears almost came into my eyes.

Then, all in a moment, I felt my inspiration. The brave, piercing notes of those cheerful small birds formed a keynote to a wonderful, light, fanciful song of hope and joy and altruism. Like myself, they were creatures with hearts pitched to the tune of woods and fields; as I was, so were they captives by circumstance in the discordant, dull city—yet with how much grace and glee they bore the restraint!

And then the early morning people began to pass through the square to their work—sullen people, with sidelong glances and glum faces, hurrying, hurrying, hurrying. And I got my theme cut out clear from the bird notes, and wrought it into a lesson, and a poem, and a carnival dance, and a lullaby; and then translated it all into prose and began to write.

For two hours my pencil traveled over my pad with scarcely a rest. Then I went to the little room I had rented for two days, and there I cut it to half, and then mailed it, white-hot, to the *Sun*.

The next morning I was up by daylight and spent two cents of my capital for a paper. If the word "sparrow" was in it I was unable to find it.

I took it up to my room and spread it out on the bed and went over it, column by column. Something was wrong.

Three hours afterward the postman brought me a large envelope containing my MS. and a piece of inexpensive paper, about 3 inches by 4—I suppose some of you have seen them—upon which was written in violet ink, "With the *Sun's* thanks."

I went over to the square and sat upon a bench. No; I did not think it necessary to eat any breakfast that morning. The confounded pests of sparrows were making the square hideous with their idiotic "cheep, cheep." I never saw birds so persistently noisy, impudent, and disagreeable in all my life.

By this time, according to all traditions, I should have been standing in the office of the editor of the *Sun*. That personage—a tall, grave, white-haired man—would strike a silver bell as he grasped my hand and wiped a suspicious moisture from his glasses.

"Mr. McChesney," he would be saying when a subordinate appeared, "this is Mr. Henry, the young man who sent in that exquisite gem about the sparrows in Madison Square. You may give him a desk at once. Your salary, sir, will be $80 a week, to begin with."

This was what I had been led to expect by all writers who have evolved romances of literary New York.

Something was decidedly wrong with tradition. I could not assume the blame; so I fixed it upon the sparrows. I began to hate them with intensity and heat.

At that moment an individual wearing an excess of whiskers, two hats, and a pestilential air slid into the seat beside me.

"Say, Willie," he muttered cajolingly, "could you cough up a dime out of your coffers for a cup of coffee this morning?"

"I'm lung-weary, my friend," said I. "The best I can do is three cents."

"And you look like a gentleman, too," said he. "What brung you down—booze?"

"Birds," I said fiercely. "The brown-throated songsters carolling songs of hope and cheer to weary man toiling amid the city's dust and din. The little feathered couriers from the meadows and woods chirping sweetly to us of blue skies and flowering fields. The confounded little squint-eyed nuisances yawping like a flock of steam pianos, and stuffing themselves like aldermen with grass seeds and bugs, while a man sits on a bench and goes without his breakfast. Yes, sir, birds! look at them!"

As I spoke I picked up a dead tree branch that lay by the bench, and hurled it with all my force into a close congregation of the sparrows on the grass. The flock flew to the trees with a babel of shrill cries; but two of them remained prostrate upon the turf.

In a moment my unsavory friend had leaped over the row of benches and secured the fluttering victims, which he thrust hurriedly into his pockets. Then he beckoned me with a dirty forefinger.

"Come on, cully," he said hoarsely. "You're in on the feed."

Weakly I followed my dingy acquaintance. He led me away from the park down a side street and through a crack in a fence into a vacant lot where some excavating had been going on. Behind a pile of old stones and lumber he paused, and took out his birds.

STANLEY FOX

"I got matches," said he. "You got any paper to start a fire with?"

I drew forth my manuscript story of the sparrows, and offered it for burnt sacrifice. There were old planks, splinters, and chips for our fire. My frowsy friend produced from some interior of his frayed clothing half a loaf of bread, pepper, and salt.

In ten minutes each of us was holding a sparrow spitted upon a stick over the leaping flames.

"Say," said my fellow bivouacker, "this ain't so bad when a fellow's hungry. It reminds me of when I struck New York first—about fifteen years ago. I come in from the West to see if I could get a job on a newspaper. I hit the Madison Square Park the first mornin' after, and was sitting around on the benches. I noticed the sparrows chirpin,' and the grass and trees so nice and green that I thought I was back in the country again. Then I got some papers out of my pocket, and—"

"I know," I interrupted. "You sent it to the *Sun* and got $15."

"Say," said my friend, suspiciously, "you seem to know a good deal. Where was you? I went to sleep on the bench there, in the sun, and somebody touched me for every cent I had—$15."

Piri Thomas
Down These Mean Streets
1967

I decided to take a long walk down Fifth Avenue, downtown to the streets of big rich buildings with cool doormen and even cooler rich men. What a smooth idea, I thought, to live right across from Central Park. I tried not to be too jealous. After all, like people said, money wasn't everything—just 99 per cent of living and one per cent of dying. Your insurance took care of the last.

I crossed Fifth Avenue and walked into the wide-open country of Central Park. What a great feeling. I struck out for the hills and picked a cool-looking tree with grass underneath it and lay down under it and chewed up the blue sky through the thick leaves. The afternoon was fading. I felt around without looking, trying to find a nice piece of twig or a blade of country Central Park grass to chew on, just like they do in the movies.

Isn't this boss, I thought, just lying here, like this was my whole world? Someday I'm gonna buy this here country Central Park—and anybody can come in, but only if they promise not to chew more than one twig or a blade of country Central Park grass. On second thought, not everybody can come in, only people like me. Along with the "No Dogs Allowed" signs, I'll have "Only People Like Me Allowed." I'll tear down the "Keep off the Grass" signs. And while I'm doing this, I might as well tear down the "No Dogs Allowed" and the "Curb Your Dogs" signs also. Maybe I'll put up "Curb Your People" signs. Man, if this is gonna be my country Central Park, I might as well do it up right. Let's see, "No Bopping Allowed" signs, or better yet:

BOPPING ALLOWED FROM

9 P.M. to 1 A.M.—MON. TO FRI.

1 A.M. to 6 P.M.—SAT.

NO BOPPING ON SUN.

LORD'S DAY

James Baldwin
Go Tell It on the Mountain
1954

In Central Park the snow had not yet melted on his favorite hill. This hill was in the center of the park, after he had left the circle of the reservoir, where he always found, outside the high wall of crossed wire, ladies, white, in fur coats, walking their great dogs, or old, white gentlemen with canes. At a point that he knew by instinct and by the shape of the buildings surrounding the park, he struck out on a steep path overgrown with trees, and climbed a short distance until he reached the clearing that led to the hill. Before him, then, the slope stretched upward, and above it the brilliant sky, and beyond it, cloudy and far away, he saw the skyline of New York. He did not know why, but there arose in him an exultation and a sense of power, and he ran up the hill like an engine, or a madman, willing to throw himself headlong into the city that glowed before him.

But when he reached the summit he paused; he stood on the crest of the hill, hands clasped beneath his chin, looking down. Then he, John, felt like a giant who might crumble this city with his anger; he felt like a tyrant who might crush this city beneath his heel; he felt like a long-awaited conquerer at whose feet flowers would be strewn, and before whom multitudes cried, Hosanna! He would be, of all, the mightiest, the most beloved, the Lord's anointed; and he would live in this shining city which his ancestors had seen with longing from far away. For it was his; the inhabitants of the city had told him it was his; he had but to run down, crying, and they would take him to their hearts and show him wonders his eyes had never seen.

And still, on the summit of that hill he paused. He remembered the people he had seen in that city, whose eyes held no love for him. And he thought of their feet so swift and brutal, and the dark gray clothes they wore, and how when they passed they did not see him, or, if they saw him, they smirked. And how their lights, unceasing, crashed on and off above him, and how he was a stranger there. Then he remembered his father and his mother, and all the arms stretched out to hold him back, to save him from this city where, they said, his soul would find perdition.

DESCRIPTIVE VIEW OF NEW YORK

The Lord supreme the basis laid
For science, commerce, and for trade;
And sent a wise and chosen race,
To build and beautify the place.

Thomas Eaton
from *Review of New York*
1814

STARS

O, sweep of stars over Harlem Streets,
O, little breath of oblivion that is night.
       A city building
       To a mother's song.
       A city dreaming
       To a lullaby.
Reach up your hand, dark boy, and take a star.
Out of the little breath of oblivion
       That is night
       Take just
       One star.

                    Langston Hughes
                    1947

TOM SCIACCA

LOUIS LOZOWICK

Anonymous

Sunshine & Shadow
1974

Between buildings that loomed like mountains we struggled with our bundles...through the swarming streets of the ghetto...I looked about the narrow streets of squeezed in stores and houses, ragged clothes, dirty bedding oozing out of the windows, ash cans ...cluttering the sidewalks. A vague sadness pressed down my heart, the first doubt of America...I looked out into the alley below and saw pale faced children scrambling in the gutter. "Where is America?" cried my heart. America, it turned out, was uptown.

Thomas Wolfe

Enchanted City
from *The Web and the Rock*
1939

Perhaps it is just here, in the iron-breasted city, that one comes closest to the enigma that haunts and curses the whole land. The city is the place where men are constantly seeking to find their door and where they are doomed to wandering forever. Of no place is this more true than of New York. Hideously ugly for the most part, one yet remembers it as a place of proud and passionate beauty; the place of everlasting hunger, it is also the place where men feel their lives will gloriously be fulfilled and their hunger fed.

In no place in the world can the life of the lonely boy, the country-man who has been drawn northwards to the flame of his lust, be more barren, more drab, more hungry and comfortless. His life is the life of subways, of rebreathed air, of the smell of burned steel, weariness and the exhausted fetidity of a cheap rented room in the apartment of "a nice couple" on 113th Street, or perhaps the triumph of an eighty-dollar apartment in Brooklyn, upper Manhattan, or the Bronx which he rents with three or four other youths. Here they "can do as they please," a romantic aspiration which leads to Saturday night parties, to cheap gin, cheap girls, to a feverish and impotent fumbling, and perhaps to an occasional distressed, drunken, and half-public fornication.

If the youth is of a serious bent, if he has thoughts of "improving" himself, there is the gigantic desolation of the Public Library, a cut-rate ticket at Gray's and a seat in the balcony of an art-theatre play that has been highly praised and that all intellectual people will be seeing, or the grey depression of a musical Sunday afternoon at Carnegie Hall, filled with arrogant-looking little musicians with silky mustaches who hiss like vipers in the dark when the works of a hated composer are played; or there is always the Metropolitan Museum....

It is therefore astonishing that nowhere in the world can a young man feel greater hope and expectancy than here. The promise of glorious fulfillment, of love, wealth, fame—or unimaginable joy—is always impending in the air. He is torn with a thousand desires and he is unable to articulate one of them, but he is sure that he will grasp joy to his heart, that he will hold love and glory in his arms, that the intangible will be touched, the inarticulate spoken, the inapprehensible apprehended; and that this may happen at any moment.

Damon Runyon, Jr.

Damon Runyon's Ashes
from *Father's Footsteps*
1953

November 17, 1946

My dear Son:

These are your instructions for the disposal of my remains and you are not to permit any one to dissuade you from them on any grounds.

Have Campbell's...take charge of body immediately on being advised of my death.

No funeral services. No display of my body. No flowers.

I desire that my body be cremated and my ashes scattered without publicity over the island of Manhattan, the place I have truly loved and that was so good to me.

I think you can get Captain Eddie Rickenbacker of Eastern Airways to get his boys to perform this service for me. If you like you may have my name added to the stone over your mother's grave in the family plot at Woodlawn.

I have often expressed these wishes about my disposition in my column and other writings so there is nothing new about them save as addressed to you personally.

In Affection,
Dad

P.S. There is a copy of these instructions in my box in the hotel office or the vault box in the Chase National Bank branch at 143 57th.

Dad

O. Henry
The Making of a New Yorker

from *The Trimmed Lamp*
1907

One day Raggles came and laid seige to the heart of the great city of Manhattan. She was the greatest of all; and he wanted to learn her note in the scale; to taste and appraise and classify and solve and label her and arrange her with the other cities that had given

him up the secret of their individuality. And here we cease to be Raggles's translator and become his chronicler.

Raggles landed from a ferry-boat one morning and walked into the core of the town with the blasé air of a cosmopolite. He was dressed with care to play the rôle of an "unidentified man." No country, race, class, clique, union, party clan, or bowling association could have claimed him. His clothing, which had been donated to him piece-meal by citizens of different heights, but same number of inches around the heart, was not yet as uncomfortable to his figure as those specimens of raiment, self-measured, that are railroaded to you by transcontinental tailors with a suit case, suspenders, silk handkerchief and pearl studs as a bonus. Without money—as a poet should be—but with the ardor of an astronomer discovering a new star in the chorus of the milky way, or a man who has seen ink suddenly flow from his fountain pen,

LOU BEACH

Raggles wandered into the great city.

Late in the afternoon he drew out of the roar and commotion with a look of dumb terror on his countenance. He was defeated, puzzled, discomfited, frightened. Other cities had been to him as long primer to read; as country maidens quickly to fathom; as send-price-of-subscription-with-answer rebuses to solve; as oyster cocktails to swallow; but here was one as cold, glittering, serene, impossible as a four-carat diamond in a window to a lover outside fingering damply in his pocket his ribbon-counter salary. . . .

The thing that weighed heaviest on Raggles's soul and clogged his poet's fancy was the spirit of absolute egotism that seemed to saturate the people as toys are saturated with paint. Each one that he considered appeared a monster of abominable and insolent conceit. Humanity was gone from them; they were toddling idols of stone and varnish, worshipping themselves and greedy for though oblivious of worship from their fellow graven images. Frozen, cruel, implacable, impervious, cut to an identical pattern, they hurried on their ways like statues brought by some miracle to motion, while soul and feeling lay unaroused in the reluctant marble.

Gradually Raggles became conscious of certain types. One was an elderly gentleman with a snow-white, short beard, pink, unwrinkled face, and stony, sharp blue eyes, attired in the fashion of a gilded youth, who seemed to personify the city's wealth, ripeness and frigid unconcern. Another type was a woman, tall, beautiful, clear as a steel engraving, goddess-like, calm, clothed like the princesses of old, with eyes as coldly blue as the reflection of sunlight on a glacier. And another was a by-product of this town of marionettes—a broad, swaggering, grim, threateningly sedate fellow, with a jowl as large as a harvested wheat field, the complexion of a baptized infant, and the knuckles of a prize-fighter. This type leaned against cigar signs and viewed the world with frappéd contumely. . . .

Raggles summoned his courage and sought alms from the populace. Unheeding, regardless, they passed on without the wink of an eyelash to testify that they were conscious of his existence. And then he said to himself that this fair but pitiless city of Manhattan was without a soul; that its inhabitants were mannikins moved by wires and springs, and that he was alone in a great wilderness.

Raggles started to cross the street. There was a blast, a roar, a hissing and a crash as something struck him and hurled him over and over six yards from where he had been. As he was coming down like the stick of a rocket the earth and all the cities thereof turned to a fractured dream.

Raggles opened his eyes. First an odor made itself known to him—an odor of the earliest spring flowers of Paradise. And then a hand soft as a falling petal touched his brow. Bending over him was the woman clothed like the princess of old, with blue eyes, now soft and humid with human sympathy. Under his head on the pavement were silks and furs. With Raggles's hat in his hand and with his face pinker than ever from a vehement outburst of oratory against reckless driving, stood the elderly gentleman who personified the city's wealth and ripeness. From a near-by café hurried the by-product with the vast jowl and baby complexion, bearing a glass full of crimson fluid that suggested delightful possibilities.

"Drink dis, sport," said the by-product, holding the glass to Raggles's lips.

Hundreds of people huddled around in a moment, their faces wearing the deepest concern. Two flattering and gorgeous policemen got into the circle and pressed back the overplus of Samaritans. An old lady in a black shawl spoke loudly of camphor; a newsboy slipped one of his papers beneath Raggles's elbow, where

it lay on the muddy pavement. A brisk young man with a notebook was asking for names.

A bell clanged importantly, and the ambulance cleaned a lane through the crowd. A cool surgeon slipped into the midst of affairs.

"How do you feel, old man?" asked the surgeon, stooping easily to his task. The princess of silks and satins wiped a red drop or two from Raggles's brow with a fragrant cobweb.

"Me?" said Raggles, with a seraphic smile, "I feel fine."

He had found the heart of his new city.

In three days they let him leave his cot for the convalescent ward in the hospital. He had been in there an hour when the attendants heard sounds of conflict. Upon investigation they found that Raggles had assaulted and damaged a brother convalescent—a glowering transient whom a freight train collision had sent in to be patched up.

"What's all this about?" inquired the head nurse.

"He was runnin' down me town," said Raggles.

"What town?" asked the nurse.

"Noo York," said Raggles.

John Lennon
Lennon Remembers
from *Rolling Stone* interview
1971

EVE CHWAST

What do you think of America?

I love it, and I hate it. America is where it's at. I should have been born in New York, I should have been born in the Village, that's where I belong. Why wasn't I born there? Paris was it in the 18th Century, London I don't think has ever been it except literary-wise when Wilde and Shaw and all of them were there. New York was it.

I regret profoundly that I was not an American and not born in Greenwich Village. That's where I should have been. It never works that way. Everybody heads toward the center, that's why I'm here now. . . .

YOKO: He's very New York, you know.

Natural History

Charles Dickens
American Notes
1842

Once more in Broadway! Here are the same ladies in bright colours, walking to and fro, in pairs and singly; yonder the very same light blue parasol which passed and repassed the hotel-window twenty times while we were sitting there. We are going to cross here. Take care of the pigs. Two portly sows are trotting up behind this carriage, and a select party of half-a-dozen gentlemen hogs have just now turned the corner.

Here is a solitary swine lounging homeward by himself. He has only one ear; having parted with the other to vagrant-dogs in the course of his city rambles. But he gets on very well without it; and leads a roving, gentlemanly, vagabond kind of life, somewhat answering to that of our club-men at home. He leaves his lodgings every morning at a certain hour, throws himself upon the town, gets through his day in some manner quite satisfactory to himself, and regularly appears at the door of his own house again at night, like the mysterious master of Gil Blas. He is a free-and-easy, careless, indifferent kind of pig, having a very large acquaintance among other pigs of the same character, whom he rather knows by sight than conversation, as he seldom troubles himself to stop and exchange civilities, but goes grunting down the kennel, turning up the news and small-talk of the city in the shape of cabbage-stalks and offal, and bearing no tails but his own: which is a very short one, for his old enemies, the dogs, have been at that too, and have left him hardly enough to swear by. He is in every respect a republican pig, going wherever he pleases, and mingling with the best society, on an equal, if not superior footing, for every one makes way when he appears, and the haughtiest give him the wall, if he prefer it. . . .

They are the city scavengers, these pigs. Ugly brutes they are; having, for the most part, scanty brown backs, like the lids of old horse-hair trunks: spotted with unwholesome black blotches. They have long, gaunt legs, too, and such peaked snouts, that if one of them could be persuaded to sit for his profile, nobody would recognise it for a pig's likeness. They are never attended upon, or fed, or driven, or caught, but are thrown upon their own resources in early life, and become preternaturally knowing in consequence. Every pig knows where he lives much better than anybody could tell him. At this hour, just as evening is closing in, you will see them roaming towards bed by scores, eating their way to the last. Occasionally, some youth among them who has over-eaten himself, or has been worried by dogs, trots shrinkingly homeward, like a prodigal son: but this is a rare case: perfect self-possession and self-reliance, and immovable composure, being their foremost attributes.

Adriaen Van der Donck
Of the Fishes
from A Description of the New Netherlands
1653

All the waters of the New Netherlands are rich with fishes. Sturgeons are plenty in the rivers at their proper season; but these fish are not esteemed, and when large are not eaten. No person takes the trouble to salt or souse them for profit; and the roes from which the costly *caviaer* is prepared, are cast away. Salmon are plenty in some rivers, and the striped bass are plenty in all the rivers and bays of the sea. The bass is a fish which in its form differs but little from the salmon. The inside of the latter is red, and of the other white. The bass are also a fine fish, and their heads are delicious food. The drums are a tolerably good fish, somewhat like the cod in form but not so stout. I have heard it said that the drums were named *Thirteens*, when the Christians first began fishing in the New Netherlands. Then every one was desirous to see the fishes which were caught, for the purpose of discovering whether the same were known to them, and if they did not know the fish, then they gave it a name. First in the fishing season they caught many shad, which they named *Elft*. Later they caught the striped bass, which they named *Twalft*. Later still they caught the drums, which they named *Dertienen*. For those fishes succeeded each other in their seasons, and the same are still known by the names which were thus derived. There are also carp, snook, forrels, pike, trout, suckers, thickheads, flounders, eels, palings, brickens, and lampreys. Some of the latter are as large as a man's leg, and above an ell in length. There are also sun-fish tasted like the perch, having small shining scales, with brilliant spots, from which they have derived the name of sun-fish. In the winter season, the creeks and backwaters abound with a small kind of fish which comes from the sea, about the size of a smelt. Some call them little mullets. Those fishes are so tame that many are caught with the hand; and as those come with the frost, we call them frost-fish. Outside at sea, and in some of the bays of the East river, the codfish are very

CENTRAL PARK

THE RAMBLE.

plenty; and if we would practice our art and experience in fishing, we could take ship loads of codfish, for it can be easily accomplished. There are also shellfish, week-fish, herrings, mackerel, roah, hallibut, scoll, and sheeps-heads. The latter are formed like the sun-fish, but much heavier, with cross stripes, being about the weight of the largest carps. They have teeth in the fore part of the mouth like a sheep, but are not voracious, and are an excellent fish. There is another species of fish, called black-fish, which are held in high estimation by the Christians. It is as brown as a *seek*, formed like the carp, but not so coarse in its scales. When this kind of fish, which are plenty, is served upon the table, it goes before all others, for every person prefers it. There are also porpoises, herring-hogs, pot-heads or sharks, turtles, &c., and whales, of which there are none caught, but if preparations were made for the purpose, then it might be easily effected; but our colonists have not advanced far enough to pursue whaling. A lost bird, however, is frequently cast and stranded, which is cut up. Lobsters are plenty in many places. Some of those are very large, being from five to six feet in length; others again are from a foot to a foot and a half long, which are the best for the table. There are also crabs, like those of the Netherlands, some of which are altogether soft.

Washington Irving
Knickerbocker's History of New York
1809

It was one of those rich autumnal days which heaven particularly bestows upon the beauteous island of Mannahata and its vicinity,—not a floating cloud obscured the azure firmament,— the sun, rolling in glorious splendor through his ethereal course, seemed to expand his honest Dutch countenance into an unusual expression of benevolence, as he smiled his evening salutation upon a city which he delights to visit with his most bounteous beams,—the very winds seemed to hold in their breaths in mute attention, lest they should ruffle the tranquillity of the hour,— and the waveless bosom of the bay presented a polished mirror, in which nature beheld herself and smiled. The standard of our city, reserved, like a choice handkerchief, for days of gala, hung motionless on the flag-staff, which forms the handle of a gigantic churn; and even the tremulous leaves of the poplar and the aspen ceased to vibrate to the breath of heaven. Everything seemed to acquiesce in the profound repose of nature. The formidable eighteen-pounders slept in the embrasures of the wooden batteries, seemingly gathering fresh strength to fight the battles of their country on the next fourth of July; the solitary drum on Governor's Island forgot to call the garrison to their shovels; the evening gun had not yet sounded its signal for all the regular well-meaning poultry throughout the country to go to roost; and the fleet of canoes, at anchor between Gibbet Island and Communipaw, slumbered on their rakes, and suffered the innocent oysters to lie for a while unmolested in the soft mud of their native banks! My own feelings sympathized with the contagious tranquillity, and I should infallibly have dozed upon one of those fragments of benches, which our benevolent magistrates have provided for the benefit of convalescent loungers, had not the extraordinary inconvenience of the couch set all repose at defiance.

ANDREZJ DUDZINSKI

Daniel Denton
A Brief Description of New York
Formerly Called New Netherlands
1670

The Fruits natural to the Island are Mulberries, Posimons, Grapes great and small, Huckelberries, Cramberries, Plums of several sorts, Rosberries and Strawberries, of which last is such abundance in June, that the Fields and Woods are died red: Which the Countrey-people perceiving, instantly arm themselves with bottles of Wine, Cream, and Sugar, and in stead of a Coat of Male, every one takes a Female upon his Horse behind him, and so rushing violently into the fields, never leave till they have disrob'd them of their red colours, and turned them into the old habit....

Yea, in May you shall see the Woods and Fields so curiously bedecke with Roses, and an innumerable multitude of delightful Flowers, not only pleasing the eye, but smell, that you may behold Nature contending with Art, and striving to equal, if not excel many Gardens in England: nay, did we know the vertue of all those Plants and Herbs growing there (which time may more discover) many are of opinion, and the Natives do affirm, that there is no disease common to the Countrey, but may be cured without Materials from other Nations.

GUY BILLOUT

Michael Gold

Jews Without Money

1930

In the livery stable on our street there was an old truck horse I loved. Every night he came home weary from work, but they did not unhitch him at once. He was made to wait for hours in the street by Vassa.

The horse was hungry. That's why he'd steal apples or bananas from the pushcarts if the peddler was napping. He was kicked and beaten for this, but it did not break him of his bad habit. They should have fed him sooner after a hard day's work. He was always neglected, and dirty, fly-bitten, gall-ridden. He was nicknamed the Ganuf—the old Thief on our street.

I stole sugar from home and gave it to him. I stroked his damp nose, gray flanks, and gray tangled mane. He shook his head, and stared at me with his large gentle eyes. He never shook his head for the other boys; they marveled at my power over Ganuf.

He was a kind, good horse, and wise in many ways. For instance: Jim Bush abused him. Jim Bush was a fiery little Irish cripple who lived by doing odd jobs for the prostitute girls. Jim Bush was a tough guy only from the waist up. His blue fireman's shirt covered massive shoulders and arms. His face was red and leathery like a middle-aged cop's. . . . his legs were shriveled like a baby's.

He cracked dirty jokes with the girls, he was genial when sober.

When he was drunk he wanted to fight every one. He would leap from his crutches at a man's throat and hang there like a bulldog, squeezing for death with his powerful hands, until beaten into unconsciousness. He always began his pugnacious debauches by abusing Ganuf the Horse.

He seemed to hate Ganuf. Why, I don't know. Maybe to show his power. Jim was the height of a boy of seven. He stood there, eyes bloodshot with liquor, mouth foaming, and shouted curses at the horse. Ganuf moved; Jim struck him over the nose with a crutch. Jim grabbed the bridle. "Back up!" he yelled, then he sawed the bit on poor Ganuf's tongue. Then he clutched the horse's nostrils and tried to tear them off.

The poor horse was patient. He looked down from his great height at the screaming little cripple, and seemed to understand. He would have kicked any one else, but I think he knew Jim Bush was a cripple.

People always marveled at this scene. I used to feel sorry for my poor horse, and imagine there were tears in his eyes.

This horse dropped at work one summer day. They loosened his harness, and slopped buckets of water over him. He managed to stand up, but was weak. He dragged the truck back to the stable. Waiting there as usual to be unhitched for his supper, he fell gasping; he died on our street.

His body bloated like a balloon. He was left for a day until the wagon came to haul him to the boneyard.

When a horse lay dead in the street that way, he was seized upon to become another plaything in the queer and terrible treasury of East Side childhood.

GEORGE BELLOWS

Walt Whitman
Give Me the Splendid Silent Sun
1867

Keep your splendid silent sun,
Keep your woods, O Nature, and the quiet places by the woods,
Keep your fields of clover and timothy, and your corn-fields
    and orchards,
Keep the blossoming buckwheat fields where the Ninth-month
    bees hum;
Give me faces and streets—give me these phantoms incessant
    and endless along the trottoirs!
Give me interminable eyes—give me women—give me
    comrades and lovers by the thousand!
Let me see new ones every day—let me hold new ones by the
    hand every day!
Give me such shows—give me the streets of Manhattan!

Paul Morand
New York
1930

The American woman, that creature hated and admired by European women, the woman with the most money in her handbag, is coming out and going into action, "ready to kill" all along her route. Very fair, peroxided, or with black-fringed brow, with plucked and painted eyebrow, lips freshly penciled and reddened, tight-fitting hat, excellently shod, with an admirable leg except for the small rubber galoshes that make her feather-footed;* her body is encased in quite a short fur coat, her eyes are childish and willful, and her pink, pink cheeks emerge from a silver-fox; the American woman makes herself supreme on the Fifth Avenue pavements with overwhelming assurance, happiness and superiority.... She goes shopping before lunching at the Ritz or the Colony Club. Pure Nordics, and many Jewesses with Oriental hips and heavier, moist eyes. All the furred fauna of the creation seem to have been butchered to clothe these women—sable, badger, gray squirrel, Persian lamb, Alaskan seal, nutria, caracul, racoon, otter, leopard, muskrat, mink...mink above all. New York was born of fur-trading, and who can forget it on a morning like this?

*M. Morand apparently refers to the unfastened arctics of a few winters ago.

CITY GREENERY

If you should happen after dark
To find yourself in Central Park,
Ignore the paths that beckon you
And hurry, hurry to the zoo,
And creep into the tiger's lair.
Frankly, you'll be safer there.

                Ogden Nash
                1947

SEYMOUR CHWAST

Edward S. Martin
The Wayfarer in New York
1909

New York is merely one of the fruits of that great tree whose roots go down in the Mississippi Valley, and whose branches spread from one ocean to the other, but the tree has no great degree of affection for its fruit. It inclines to think that the big apple gets a disproportionate share of the national sap. It is disturbed by the enormous drawing power of a metropolis which constantly attracts to itself wealth and its possessors from all the lesser centers of the land. Every city, every State pays an annual tribute of men and of business to New York, and no State or city likes particularly to do it.

GREGOR SAMSA IN AMERICA   NEW YORK - NIGHT II

ROBERT ANDREW PARKER

Edward Field

Roaches
1953

An old decrepit city like London
doesn't have any.
They ought to love it there
in those smelly, elegant buildings.
Surely I myself have smuggled some in my luggage
but they obviously don't like the English—
for that alone I should love them.

They are among the brightest
and most attractive of small creatures
though you have to be prepared
for the look of horror
on the faces of out-of-town guests
when a large roach walks across the floor
as you are sipping drinks.
You reach out and swat,
and keeping the conversation going
pick up the corpse and drop it into an ashtray
feeling very New Yorky doing it.
After all, you've got to be tough to live here—
the visitor didn't make it.

Roaches also thrive on it here:
They set up lively communes
in open boxes of rice, spaghetti, and matzohs.
You come in to make coffee in the morning
and find a dead one floating in the kettle
and dots of roach shit on the dishes,
hinting at roachy revels the night before.

If you let them alone
they stop running at the sight of you
and whisker about
taking a certain interest in whatever you are doing,
and the little ones, expecting like all babies to be adored,
frolic innocently in the sink,
even in daytime when grownup roaches rest
after a night of swarming around the garbage bag.
The trouble with this approach is
they outbreed you and take over,
even moving sociably right into your bed.

Which brings up the question, Do they bite?
Some say yes, and if yes,
do they carry oriental diseases?
Even though you have tried to accept them
there comes a point when you find your eyes
studying labels of roach killers on supermarket shelves,
decide to try a minimal approach, buy one,
but when you attack with spray can aimed
they quickly learn to flee.
The fastest of course live to multiply
so they get cleverer all the time
with kamikaze leaping into space,
or zigzagging away,

race into far corners of the apartment
where they drop egg-sacks in their last throes
and start ineradicable new colonies.

When you light the oven
they come out and dance on the hot stove top
clinging with the tips of their toes,
surviving by quick footwork until you swat them.
Or if you spray it first
you have the smell of roaches roasting slowly.

And when you wash them down the drain
without their being certifiably dead
do they crawl up when the coast is clear?
Some even survive the deadliest poisons devised by man
and you have weird, white mutations running about.
Dying, they climb the walls, or up your legs, in agony,
making you feel like a dirty rat,
until they fall upside down with frail legs
waving in the air.

No more half-measures—
it's them or us you finally realize
and decide on nothing less than total fumigation:
The man comes while you are out
and you return to a silent apartment, blissfully roach-free.
You vacuum up the scattered bodies of the unlucky,
pushing down guilty feelings, lonely feelings,
and congratulate yourself.

                                        You booby,
they have only moved over to the neighbor's
and she too is forced to fumigate,
and just when you are on the princess phone crowing to your
        friends,
back they come, the whole tribe of them,
many gone now
due to their trivial life-span and chemical adversaries
but more numerous than ever with the new born
and all the relatives from next door and the neighborhood with
        them,
you standing there outraged, but secretly relieved
as they swarm into the kitchen from every crevice,
glad to be home, the eternal innocents,
greeting you joyfully.

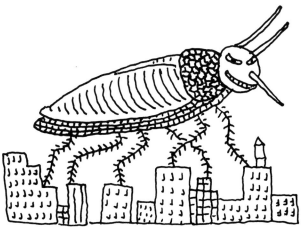

SEYMOUR CHWAST

Herman Melville
Moby-Dick
1851

There now is your insular city of the Manhattoes, belted round by wharves as Indian isles by coral reefs—commerce surrounds it with her surf. Right and left, the streets take you waterward. Its extreme down-town is the Battery, where that noble mole is washed by waves, and cooled by breezes, which a few hours previous were out of sight of land. Look at the crowds of water-gazers there.

Circumambulate the city on a dreamy Sabbath afternoon. Go from Corlears Hook to Coenties Slip, and from thence, by Whitehall, northward. What do you see?—Posted like silent sentinels all around the town, stand thousands upon thousands of mortal men fixed in ocean reveries. Some leaning against the spiles; some seated upon the pier-heads; some looking over the bulwarks of ships from China; some high aloft in the rigging, as if striving to get a still better seaward peep. But these are all landsman; of week days pent up in lath and plaster—tied to counters, nailed to benches, clinched to desks. How then is this? Are the green fields gone? What do they here?

But look! here come more crowds, pacing straight for the water, and seemingly bound for a dive. Strange! Nothing will content them but the extremest limit of the land; loitering under the shady lee of yonder warehouses will not suffice. No. They must get just as nigh the water as they possibly can without falling in. And there they stand—miles of them—leagues. Inlanders all, they come from lanes and alleys, streets and avenues—north, east, south, and west. Yet here they all unite. Tell me, does the magnetic virtue of the needles of the compasses of all those ships attract them thither?

Joseph Mitchell
Old Mr. Flood
1948

The fish market supports a flock of four or five hundred gulls and at least two dozen of them are one-legged. "This condition," Mr. Flood says, "is due to the fact that sea gulls don't understand traffic lights. There's a stretch of South Street running through the market that's paved with cobblestones. And every so often during the morning rush a fish drops off a truck and is ground up by the wheels and packed down tight into the cracks between the cobbles. The gulls go wild when they see this. They wait until traffic gets halted by a red light, and then they drop out of the sky like bats out of hell and try to pull and worry the fish from between the cobbles. They're stubborn birds. They get so interested they don't notice when the light changes and all of a sudden, wham bang, the heavy truck traffic is right on top of them. Some get killed outright. Some get broken wings and flop off and hide somewhere and starve to death. Those that lose only one leg are able to keep going, but the other gulls peck them and claw them and treat them as outcasts and they have a hard, hard time." The gimpy gulls are extremely distrustful, but Mr. Flood has been able to make friends with a few. . . . One or two will eat from his hands.

SEYMOUR CHWAST

Brander Matthews
Outlines in Local Color
1898

As he came down the steps of his sister's little house, that first Saturday in May, he saw before him the fresh greenery of the grass in Stuyvesant Square and the delicate blossoms on its sparse bushes and the young leaves on its trees; and he felt in himself also the subtle influences of the spring-tide. The sky was cloudless, serene, and unfathomably blue. The sun shone clearly, and the shadows it cast were already lengthening along the street. The gentle breeze blew hesitatingly. He heard the inarticulate shriek of the hawker bearing a tray containing a dozen square boxes of strawberries and walking near a cart piled high with crates. When he crossed Third Avenue he noticed that a white umbrella had flowered out over the raised chair of the Italian boot-black at the corner. A butcher-boy, with basket on arm, was lingering at a basement door in lively banter with a good-looking Irish cook. A country wagon, full of growing plants, crawled down the street while the vender bawled forth the cheapness of his wares.

There were other signs of the season at Union Square—the dingy landaus with their tops half open, the flowers bedded out in bright profusion, the aquatic plants adorning the broad basin of the fountain, the pigeons wooing and cooing languidly, the sparrows energetically flirting and fighting, the young men and maidens walking slowly along the curving paths and smiling in each other's faces. To Harry Grant, just home from a long winter in the bleak Northwest, it seemed as though man and nature were alike rejoicing in the rising of the sap and the bourgeoning of spring. It was as though the pulse of the strong city were beating more swiftly and with renewed youth. Harry Grant felt his own heart rejoice that he was back again amid the sights he loved, within a stone's-throw of the house where he was born, within pistol-shot of the residence of the girl he was now going at last to ask to marry him.

Thomas Wolfe
Enchanted City
from *The Web and the Rock*
1939

. . . there is always the feeling that the earth is full of gold, and that who will seek and strive can mine it.

In New York there are certain wonderful seasons in which this feeling grows to a lyrical intensity. One of these are those first tender days of Spring when lovely girls and women seem suddenly to burst out of the pavements like flowers: all at once the street is peopled with them, walking along with a proud, undulant rhythm of breasts and buttocks and a look of passionate tenderness on their faces. Another season is early Autumn, in October, when the city begins to take on a magnificent flash and sparkle: there are swift whippings of bright wind, a flare of bitter leaves, the smell of frost and harvest in the air; after the enervation of Summer, the place awakens to an electric vitality, the beautiful women have come back from Europe or from the summer resorts, and the air is charged with exultancy and joy.

Finally, there is a wonderful, secret thrill of some impending ecstasy on a frozen Winter's night. On one of these nights of frozen silence when the cold is so intense that it numbs one's flesh, and the sky above the city flashes with one deep jewelry of cold stars, the whole city, no matter how ugly its parts may be, becomes a proud, passionate, Northern place: everything about it seems to soar up with an aspirant, vertical, glittering magnificence to meet the stars. One hears the hoarse notes of the great ships in the river, and one remembers suddenly the princely girdle of proud, potent tides that bind the city, and suddenly New York blazes like a magnificent jewel in its fit setting of sea, and earth, and stars.

Appleton's Dictionary of New York City
1879

Bird- and Dog-Fanciers.—Places where the common song birds, such as the canary, bullfinch, skylark, and linnet, may be bought can be found in all the principal retail business streets of the city, but whoever is in quest of the more rare kinds will generally have to visit several dealers before meeting with what he wants. Dealers in dogs who have a permanent and accessible place of business are quite rare, however, and with one or two exceptions are not such as one would like to visit out of mere curiosity. An idea of the average character of these places may readily be got by a visit, say to Harry Jennings's place, 255 Centre st., where several good-sized rooms are given over entirely to a very heterogeneous collection of dogs, pigeons, white rats and mice, fancy fowl, parrots, etc. Bird- and dog-fanciers can be found in Canal st. west, in South 5th av., and also in 4th av., below 14th st., and in 6th av.; at 55 Chatham st., at 1212 and 1235 Broadway. Their advertisements will also be found in the daily papers. The prices of dogs vary of course with the age, breed, and individual excellence—in fact there is almost as great a range as there is in the price of horses. For birds, there is, however, a pretty uniform scale of prices for each kind, with a considerable range according to the accomplishments of the birds. An untrained male canary of the Hartz mountain breed—the best songsters—sells for instance for about $3, but, if the same bird has been taught to pipe a tune perfectly, as much as $50 is asked for it. Between these two extremes can be purchased others, the price of which fluctuates with the degree of perfection they have attained in the mastering of a tune. Uneducated bullfinches likewise sell for but little more than canaries that have not been trained, but when a bullfinch has succeeded in mastering three distinct tunes, as sometimes happens, $100 is the price put on him. Nightingales and other birds which will learn no melody but their own do not vary so much in price—an ordinary nightingale selling for $10, while the very best can be bought for $25. In buying it is always best to go to some responsible dealer; the canaries which are constantly hawked about the streets at a very low price, $1 or less each, are invariably females and entirely useless as songsters. In case of the illness of a dog the best place to secure proper medical attention for it is the American Veterinary Hospital, which see under the title HOSPITALS.

Betty Smith
A Tree Grows in Brooklyn
1943

The one tree in Francie's yard was neither a pine nor a hemlock. It had pointed leaves which grew along green switches which radiated from the bough and made a tree which looked like a lot of opened green umbrellas. Some people called it the Tree of Heaven. No matter where its seed fell, it made a tree which struggled to reach the sky. It grew in boarded-up lots and out of neglected rubbish heaps and it was the only tree that grew out of cement. It grew lushly, but only in the tenement districts.

You took a walk on a Sunday afternoon and came to a nice neighborhood, very refined. You saw a small one of these trees through the iron gate leading to someone's yard and you knew that soon that section of Brooklyn would get to be a tenement district. The tree knew. It came there first. Afterwards, poor foreigners seeped in and the quiet old brownstone houses were hacked up into flats, feather beds were pushed out on the window sills to air and the Tree of Heaven flourished. That was the kind of tree it was. It liked poor people.

That was the kind of tree in Francie's yard. Its umbrellas curled over, around and under her third-floor fire-escape. An eleven-year-old girl sitting on this fire-escape could imagine that she was living in a tree. That's what Francie imagined every Saturday afternoon in summer.

Joseph Mitchell

The Rivermen

from *The Bottom of the Harbor*
1959

I often feel drawn to the Hudson River, and I have spent a lot of time through the years poking around the part of it that flows past the city. I never get tired of looking at it; it hypnotizes me. I like to look at it in midsummer, when it is warm and dirty and drowsy, and I like to look at it in January, when it is carrying ice. I like to look at it when it is stirred up, when a northeast wind is blowing and a strong tide is running—a new-moon tide or a full-moon tide—and I like to look at it when it is slack. It is exciting to me on weekdays, when it is crowded with ocean craft, harbor craft, and river craft, but it is the river itself that draws me, and not the shipping, and I guess I like it best on Sundays, when there are lulls that sometimes last as long as half an hour, during which, all the way from the Battery to the George Washington Bridge, nothing moves upon it, not even a ferry, not even a tug, and it becomes as hushed and dark and secret and remote and unreal as a river in a dream.

Michael Gold

Jews Without Money

1930

Let me tell of a trait we boys showed: the hunger for country things.

New York is a devil's dream, the most urbanized city in the world. It is all geometry angles and stone. It is mythical, a city buried by a volcano. No grass is found in this petrified city, no big living trees, no flowers, no bird but the drab little lecherous sparrow, no soil, loam, earth; fresh earth to smell, earth to walk on, to roll on, and love like a woman.

Just stone. It is the ruins of Pompeii, except that seven million animals full of earth-love must dwell in the dead lava streets.

Each week at public school there was an hour called Nature Study. The old maid teacher fetched from a dark closet a collection of banal objects: birdnests, cornstalks, minerals, autumn leaves and other poor withered corpses. On these she lectured tediously, and bade us admire Nature.

What an insult. We twisted on our benches, and ached for the outdoors. It was as if a starving bum were offered snapshots of food, and expected to feel grateful. It was like lecturing a cage of young monkeys on the jungle joys.

"Lady, gimme a flower! Gimme a flower! Me, me, me!"

In summer, if a slummer or settlement house lady walked on our street with flowers in her hand, we attacked her, begging for the flowers. We rioted and yelled, yanked at her skirt, and frightened her to the point of hysteria.

Once Jake Gottlieb and I discovered grass struggling between the sidewalk cracks near the livery stable. We were amazed by this miracle. We guarded this treasure, allowed no one to step on it. Every hour the gang studied "our" grass, to try to catch it growing. It died, of course, after a few days; only children are hardy enough to grow on the East Side.

Adriaen Van der Donck

Of the Air

from *A Description of the New Netherlands*
1653

The sweet ruler that influences the wisdom, power, and appearance of man, of animals, and of plants, is the air. Many name it the temperament, or the climate. The air in the New Netherlands is so dry, sweet, and healthy that we need not wish that it were otherwise. In purity, agreeableness, and fineness, it would be folly to seek for an example of it in any other country.

Philip Hone

Diary of Philip Hone

1835

April 10.—The weather being fine and spring-like, I walked for an hour before dinner with my wife on the Battery. Strange as it is, I do not think that either of us had done such a thing in the last seven years; and what a beautiful spot it is! The grounds are in fine order; the noble bay, with the opposite shores of New Jersey, Staten and Long Islands, vessels of every description, from the noble, well-appointed Liverpool packet to the little market craft, and steamers arriving from every point, give life and animation to a prospect unexcelled by any city view in the world. It would be worth travelling one hundred miles out of one's way in a foreign country to get a sight of, and yet we citizens of New York, who have it all under our noses, seldom enjoy it. Like all other enjoyments, it loses its value from being too easily obtained.

James Kirke Paulding
The Narrows and New York Bay

from *New Mirror for Travellers; and Guide to the Springs*
1828

O it's delightful to travel, Maria! We had such a delightful sail in the steam boat, though we were all sick; and such a delightful party, if they only had been well. Only think of sailing without sails, and not caring which way the wind blows; and going eight miles an hour let what would happen. It was quite charming; but for all this I was glad when it was over, and we came into still water. Coming into the Narrows, as they are called, was like entering a Paradise. On one side is Long Island, with its low shores, studded with pretty houses, and foliage of various kinds, mixed up with the dark cedars. On the other, Staten Island, with its high bluff, crowned by the telegraph and signal poles; and beyond, the great fort that put me in mind of the old castles which Stephen talks about. We kept close to the Long Island shore, along which we glided, before wind and tide with the swiftness of wings. Every moment some new beauty opened to our view. The little islands of the bay crowned with castles; the river beyond terminated by the lofty ledge of perpendicular rocks, called the palisades; and lastly, the queen of the west, the beautiful city, with its Battery and hundred spires, all coming one after the other in succession, and at last all combined in one beautiful whole, threw me almost into raptures, and entirely cured my sea sickness. Add to this, the ships, vessels and boats, of all sizes, from the seventy-four to the little thing darting about, like a feather, with a single person in it; and the grand opening of the East River, with Brooklyn and the charming scenery beyond, and you can form some little idea of my surprise and delight....

Thomas De Voe
The Market Assistant
1867

Black bear.—The flesh of this animal is the only species I ever knew to be brought to our markets for sale. Bear, or b'ar-meat, is the common name used to designate its flesh (when spoken of), and it is rather luscious but savory eating; that from a young bear, when nearly full-grown and fat, is considered best. Generally found in our large markets in the late fall or winter months, and some years in great plenty. The dealers in its flesh cut it to suit purchasers, for roasting, steaks, etc.

The taking of one of these animals in swimming across the Hudson River, about the period of the Revolution, and exposing its body for sale in an old market, then known as Hudson-market, which stood on Greenwich-street, east (one block) of the present Washington-market, changed its name to that of the once well-known Bear-market....

The following will give some idea of their plentifulness in our State, and especially along the Hudson River, at an early period. The New York *Gazette*, October 8, 1759, has recorded—"A gentleman, who came down in one of the last sloops from Albany, says that he was ashore at several places on each side of the North River, and that at every place he landed there were great complaints made of the damage done by bears. Some complain of the loss of their sheep, hogs, and calves; others, of their devouring their fields of Indian-corn, and adding that they are more numerous than has been known in the memory of man. And, particularly, he was at a tavern on the post-road, near Poughkeepsie, when the landlord counted to him thirty-six, that had been killed within three weeks of that time, in the compass of four or five miles. Whilst this gentleman and the captain were ashore at this tavern, two bears came out of the bushes where the captain and himself landed, and swam across the river, passing very near the head of the sloop; but the battoe being ashore, it was not in the power of the people of the sloop to pursue them."

Meyer Berger
Meyer Berger's New York
1960

April 23, 1958

There is a green world high above the pavement that city groundlings rarely see. Familiar and exotic growths flourish in this sky acreage. The same birds, insects and crawling things that invade open countryside plantings climb to apartment house and skyscraper gardens—as high as thirty-eight floors at Radio City—to rob or destroy crops.

The rural housewife who puts up jams, jellies and preserves from the fruits of farm acreage has a silk-gowned bediamonded sister in town who loves to fill Mason jars and cans with penthouse-grown fruits and berries—when she doesn't have the hired cook do it.

The green-thumbed sisterhood—better than 95 per cent of the tillers of penthouse soil are women—organized the Rooftop Gardeners six years ago. The movement was started by Mrs. Carolyn Hannig, who lives atop 875 Park Avenue and runs the world's largest sand-processing industry.

She got the notion at lectures given by the New York Horticultural Society in 1952. It came to her at one of the sessions that while she could study and enjoy neighborhood penthouse gardens, she knew none of her sky neighbors. She suggested that they meet and exchange ideas, and they snapped at it.

Membership in the Rooftop Gardeners is thirty right now, with the committee considering 101 new applications. These are only a small portion of the 2,500 to 3,000 New Yorkers who use the short-sized rake and hoe on skyline acreage. Many are rich, many are humble.

The busiest and most knowledgeable top-floor husbandman is Hal Lee, a freelance writer on horticulture. He has more than 2,000 plantings on the eleventh floor at 1394 Lexington Avenue, near Ninety-second Street. His crop includes figs, bananas, strawberries, peaches, cherries. He maintains a rich compost heap of leaf mold and kitchen leavings.

Mr. Lee has worked his Lexington Avenue soil the last eleven years. When the Rooftop Gardeners organized they made him president. By and by, though, he turned professional consultant. He wanted to resign then, on the ground that he was a pro, but the resignation was unanimously rejected. He still gets all their business.

Pioneer of the penthouse Maud Mullers is Mrs. Harry Schwartz. She has kept up her penthouse garden atop 944 Fifth Avenue a full thirty-five years. She owns the tallest penthouse trees—a forty-foot honey locust, wide-branched Russian olive growths, magnolias, fifteen-foot high privet hedge and white birch, peach, apple and cherry trees, among others.

The Schwartzes, like most other crow's-nest horticulturists, grow thousands of annuals and perennials. They put their fruits and berries up in jars. They fight off crows, woodpeckers, bats, pigeons, aphids, tent caterpillars and go after all sorts of crawlers with spray guns. They grow magnificent orchids. Their pet dachshund, Penny, cremated, sleeps inside a miniature grave fence under an olive tree.

The Rooftop Gardeners eat under whispering leaves with flower scent drifting across their candle-lit tables. Some sleep in their gardens, under the stars. Some have forsaken the country entirely; just live on their green roofs. One gentleman, a United Nations delegate, has worked a broad putting-green into his garden scheme.

The secret of sky gardening seems to be peat moss. It overcomes the drying effects of lofty winds. Mr. Lee says that dampness from roof-top soil and plantings acts as a humectant—keeps a woman's complexion smooth and soft. He got that from Mrs. Lee, an expert on beauty.

And there's an advantage in having neighbors under you when you're gardening. Last spring Mr. Lee got a telephone call from a tenant three flights down. The man said: "Mr. Lee, get your spray gun handy. Tent caterpillars just passed my window, headed up." It took another hour or so, but Mr. Lee met the invasion at the parapet. The tent caterpillars never established a roof beachhead.

JAMES GRASHOW

On the Rise

Thomas Wolfe

Enchanted City

from *The Web and the Rock*
1939

Again, there is something spurious and unreal in almost all attempts at established life in the city. When one enters the neat little apartment of a young man or a young married couple, and sees there on neat, gaily-painted shelves neat rows of books—the solid little squares of the Everyman, and the Modern Library, the D. H. Lawrence, the *Buddenbrooks,* the Cabell, the art edition of *Penguin Island,* then a few of the paper-backed French books, the Proust and the Gide, and so on—one feels a sense of embarrassment and shame: there is something fraudulent about it. One feels this also in the homes of wealthy people, whether they live in a "charming little house" on Ninth Street which they have rented, or in the massive rooms of a Park Avenue apartment.

No matter what atmosphere of usage, servants, habitude, ease, and solid establishment there may be, one always has this same feeling that the thing is fraudulent, that the effort to achieve permanence in this impermanent and constantly changing life is no more real than the suggested permanence in a theatrical setting: one would not be surprised to return the next morning and find the scene dismantled, the stage bare, and the actors departed. Sometimes even the simplest social acts—the act of visiting one's friends, of talking to them in a room, of sitting around a hearthfire with them—oh, above all else, of sitting around a hearth-fire in an apartment in the city!—seem naked and pitiful. There is an enormous sadness and wistfulness about these attempts to simulate an established life in a place where the one permanent thing is change itself.

Joe Madden

And Now, Good Night

from *Who the Hell Cares?*
1948

Progress has come to our old neighborhood, the Chelsea Village. A guy will go back to the scene of his crime. That's me.

The other A.M. I packed four stogies in my kick and started on one of those walks. New York is mighty lonesome at 2 A.M. I wandered down 5th Ave. The university club at 54th St. was dark.... On down 53rd to St. Thomas' famous church whose chimes and bells on Sunday wake me as I live down the block.... Porters in all the stores mopping and cleaning...

52nd St.... the upper half owned by the Rockefellers, where a new 40-story building is just completed... across on the East Side the famous Cartier's jewelry house... the tower clock saying it was 2:10 A.M.... passed the new Best Dept. store... the famous St. Patrick's Cathedral, where yours truly worships his God, the 2-million-dollar renovation job recently finished after 2½ years ... down to 42nd Street and 5th... the famous and great public library and in back of it Bryant Park where the poets and fairies and bums repose and sleep in the good old summertime....

I keep on going to 39th St.... Kress's store, at one time the Wendell Estate... Lord & Taylor's... on down to 34th St.... B. Altman's, Empire State Building... down to 25th St.... Madison Square Park and the Eternal light where yours truly came over to look and gaze at the great big Xmas tree at Xmas time. (We in the poor sections could never afford one.)

The War Statue on 25th St.... there Tom Noonan of the famous Bowery Mission held forth rain, hail, snow or summer, handing out flop tickets... the unfortunates we call bums... he knew them and they knew him... before he went down to Doyers St. and opened the old Chinese theater as a mission...

As I got to 23rd St. I looked at the famous Flat Iron building. ... When I was a little squirt it was the tallest building in New York—23 stories high. Across the street is the site of the old Bartholdi Hotel—a famous joint for the fight and sporting crowd in the old days—now loaded with small stores, frankfurter stands, etc. Across 23rd St. west towards 8th Ave., at 6th was the home of the Masonic lodge, a big building... the good restaurants such as Adams, Zimmerman's, Shanley's, etc.... all gone. In the middle of the block the famous Keith Theatre... likewise gone... at 7th & 8th Ave. the old Chelsea Hotel is still there, also the Y.M.C.A.

On 8th Ave. where yours truly spent his youthful days hanging around the corner in front of Bachelder's Restaurant, that too is gone as is the Oak Cabaret of 30 years ago but the Old Grand Opera House where I saw many a great Bway show in the pit for two bits is still there. Later on I used to help the late Bill Dwyer as a bouncer. Bill, during Prohibition, became the biggest in the country... the nicest, sweetest guy in the world... he made millions ... died without a dime... he liked to gamble.... Terry McGovern was the ticket-taker....

Down 8th Ave. to 21st in the middle of the block No. 320 is a school now. For 35 years we lived in the old house. In the back of us was an open lot and a small warehouse storing ballot boxes and the election curtains.... We were the caretakers... our rent was $15 a month when the Democrats was in power... and $30 when the Republicans elected a Mayor. I walked down and stood in front of the school... I guess I looked like a prowler... many a thought went thru my mind....

We have some bad boys in our midst: Linky Mitchell, Rubber Shaw, One-Eyed Lynch, who went to the electric chair for killing a Cop in a mail robbery, Paddy Keenan, who got life for killing a soldier for no reason in Shield's Saloon and when he got to Sing Sing started that great big fire that lasted for 5 days. (He's still there after 30 years, if I'm not mistaken.)

Down 8th again and on to 20th where McAleenans' hock shop stood, the spot where I used to hock a five dollar watch for a deuce

S. L. MARGOLIES

PEARL ST.

THE GEM

A.C. BURR,

HOMŒOPATHIC MEDICINES
&
BOOKS.
Wm RADDE.

324   322

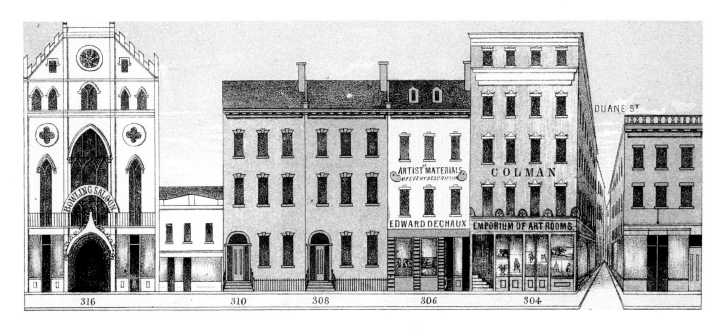

BOWLING SALOON

ARTISTS' MATERIALS
OF EVERY DESCRIPTION

COLMAN

EDWARD DECHAUX   EMPORIUM OF ART ROOMS.

DUANE ST.

316   310   308   306   304

SPINNING, BOOKBINDER &
PAPER RULER

PIERCE'S RANGES

300   298   296   294   292   290

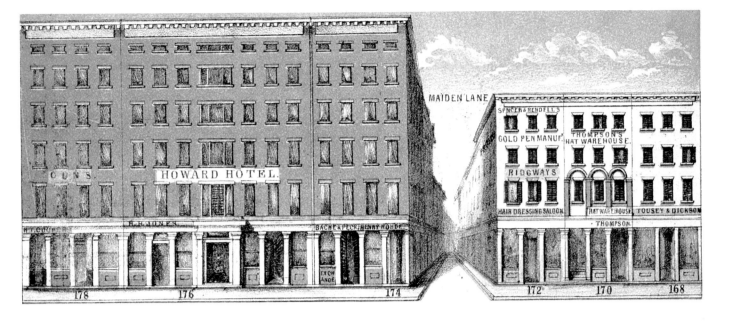

C.N.S.   HOWARD HOTEL.   MAIDEN LANE

H.T.COOPER   H.R.JONES   BACHE & PECK   HENRY ROHDE   EXCHANGE

SPENCER & RENDELL'S GOLD PEN MANUF.   THOMPSON'S HAT WAREHOUSE.

RIDGWAYS

HAIR DRESSING SALOON   HAT WAREHOUSE   TOUSEY & DICKSON

THOMPSON.

178   176   174   172   170   168

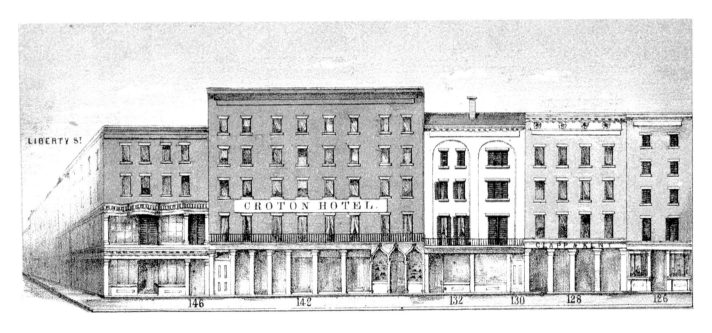

LIBERTY ST.   CROTON HOTEL.   CLAPP & KENT

146   142   132   130   128   126

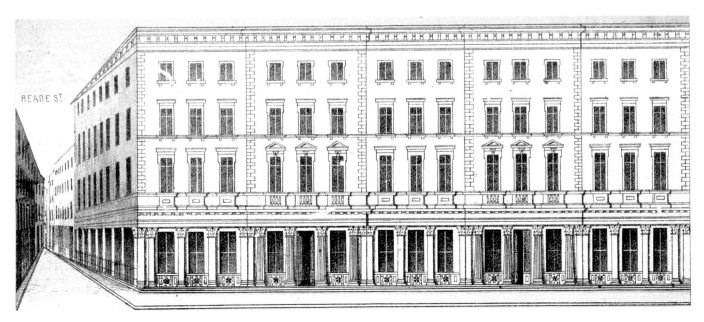

READE ST.

weekly... good ole Dinny Sheehan smiling every time I walked in.... Across the street the Old Village Theatre where we used to see all the good old silent movies for a dime.... When they raised it to 15¢ we tore the joint apart.... Down the way at 19th was the old Stephen Merritt Funeral Parlor, later taken over by Hershey's Chocolates.... I stopped there, as I was getting sadder and sadder.... All these places are torn down.... They have big apartment buildings now.... All the old families and the guys I hung out with are all gone....

The old Chelsea Village aint what it used to be. Gone are the old landmarks—Cushman's Bakery where we got a full bag of hot crullers for a dime... the old Pasteur Institute, that's gone too. The old homes that used to have fences and trees... and the houses that were 100 feet back are gone too. Now we have the famous London Terrace Apartments there....

I was going to walk down to the old 23rd St. Ferry where I used to hustle baggage, but it was 5 A.M. so I wandered back to 8th Ave. again to get the subway. I passed the drugstore next to the Cornish Arms Hotel where some of our nice Sunday school boys cut Vincent Coll the mad dog killer in two with machine gun bullets one summer evening years ago....

So, folks, progress has hit my old neighborhood, the same as yours.... Chelsea Village don't look the same... it ain't the same... it is a spot I loved and I will never forget it... as it was....

Good night....

James Fenimore Cooper
Home as Found
1832

"Here, then, you may suit yourself with any species of real estate that heart can desire. If a villa is wanted, there are a dozen. Of farms a hundred are in market; that is merely half a dozen streets; and here are towns, of dimensions and value to suit purchasers."

"Explain this. It exceeds comprehension."

"It is simply what it professes to be. Mr. Hammer, do us the favor to step this way. Are you selling to-day?"

"Not much, sir. Only a hundred or two lots on this island, and some six or eight farms, with one Western village."

"Can you tell us the history of this particular piece of property, Mr. Hammer?"

"With great pleasure, Mr. Effingham; we know you to have means, and hope you may be induced to purchase. This was the farm of old Volkert Van Brunt, five years since, off of which he and his family had made a livelihood for more than a century, by selling milk. Two years since, the sons sold it to Peter Feeler for a hundred an acre, or for the total sum of five thousand dollars. The next spring Mr. Feeler sold it to John Search, as keen a one as we have, for twenty-five thousand. Search sold it at private sale to Nathan Rise for fifty thousand the next week, and Rise had parted with it to a company, before the purchase, for a hundred and twelve thousand, cash. The map ought to be taken down—for it is now eight months since we sold it out in lots, at auction, for the gross sum of three hundred thousand dollars. As we have received our commission, we look at that land as out of the market for a time."

"Have you other property, sir, that affords the same wonderful history of a rapid advance in value?" asked the baronet.

"These walls are covered with maps of estates in the same predi-

cament. Some have risen two or three thousand per cent. within five years, and some only a few hundred. There is no calculating in the matter—for it is all fancy."

"And on what is this enormous increase in value founded? Does the town extend to these fields?"

"It goes much farther, sir; that is to say, on paper. In the way of houses, it is still some miles short of them. A good deal depends on what you call a thing, in this market. Now, if old Volkert Van Brunt's property had been still called a farm, it would have brought a farm price; but, as soon as it was surveyed into lots, and mapped—"

"Mapped!"

"Yes, sir; brought into visible lines, with feet and inches. As soon as it was properly mapped, it rose to its just value. We have a good deal of the bottom of the sea that brings fair prices in consequence of being well mapped."

Here the gentlemen expressed their sense of the auctioneer's politeness, and retired.

"We will now go into the sales-room," said John Effingham, "where you shall judge of the spirit, or energy, as it is termed, which at this moment actuates this great nation."

Descending, they entered a crowd, where scores were eagerly bidding against each other, in the fearful delusion of growing rich by pushing a fancied value to a point still higher. One was purchasing ragged rocks, another the bottom of rivers, a third a bog, and all on the credit of maps. Our two observers remained some time silent spectators of the scene.

"When I first entered that room," said John Effingham, as they left the place, "it appeared to me to be filled with maniacs. Now, that I have been in it several times, the impression is not much altered."

Felix Riesenberg
East Side, West Side
1927

In the springtime of the city, the greater and greater city of New York, Becka, in the slightly better summer dress she had bought the day before, and John, fairly presentable, with much help from Becka, the money equally divided between them, for safe keeping, rode uptown, far uptown on the subway.

"I want to get as far from the noise of the Bowery and the smell of Fifth Avenue as we can go." John pulled Becka out of the tube at 168th Street; they walked toward the river. New shiny apartment houses were being built.

"Gee, I ain't never been this far, John. Ain't it swell. It's expensive up here, I bet."

"There's three thousand in the bank, Becka. We'll get a start. Let's look in here." They went into an ornate hall, a truly magnificent entrance way with a terrazzo floor and period chairs and table. Several apartments fortunately were still for lease.

"Oh, John—look, look." Out through the back window was a superb view of the Hudson. "Look," then she was standing in the door of a bathroom; snow white tiles and an enameled tub; and shiny new nickel-plated faucets, running hot and cold water. A living room, a tiny kitchen, a bed room and bath. "Oh, John— ain't this grand!"

"Only fifty a month, sir." The agent was almost apologetic.

"Suits me. How about you?" Becka nodded. "All right, I'll take

"That superintendent sent up ice." The little refrigerator was cold. The new gas stove was humming, John had put a quarter in the meter. Becka, with amazing dexterity, had a pot roast under way in the oven, and a pan of hot biscuits followed.

"Where'd you learn all this?" John was utterly astonished.

"Say! you think I'm green. I had a little experience keeping house. Not in a swell place like this, but I know a thing or two, Mr. John."

H. C. Bunner
The Story of a New York House
1887

Mr. Dolph continued on his walk up Broadway. As he passed the upper end of the Common he looked with interest at the piles of red sandstone among the piles of white marble, where they were building the new City Hall. The Council had ordered that the rear or northward end of the edifice should be constructed of red stone; because red stone was cheap, and none but a few suburbans would ever look down on it from above Chambers Street. Mr. Dolph shook his head. He thought he knew better. He had watched the growth of trade; he knew the room for further growth; he had noticed the long converging lines of river-front, with their unbounded accommodation for wharves and slips. He believed that the day would come—and his own boy might see it—when the business of the city would crowd the dwelling-houses from the river side, east and west, as far, maybe, as Chambers Street. He had no doubt that the boy might find himself, forty years from then, in a populous and genteel neighborhood. Perhaps he foresaw too much; but he had a jealous yearning for a house that should be a home for him, and for his child, and for his grandchildren. He wanted a place where his wife might have a garden; a place which the boy would grow up to love and cherish, where the boy might bring a wife some day. And even if it were a little out of town—why, his wife did not want a rout every night; and it was likely his old friends would come out and see him once in a while, and smoke a pipe in his garden and eat a dish of strawberries, perhaps.

As he thought it all over for the hundredth time, weighing for and against in his gentle and deliberative mind, he strolled far out of town. There was a house here and there on the road—a house with a trim, stiff little garden, full of pink and white and blue flowers in orderly, clam-shell-bordered beds. But it was certainly, he had to admit, as he looked about him, very *countrified* indeed. It seemed that the city must lose itself if it wandered up here among these rolling meadows and wooded hills. Yet even up here, half way to Greenwich Village, there were little outposts of the town—clumps of neighborly houses, mostly of the poorer class, huddling together to form small nuclei for sporadic growth. There was one on his right, near the head of Collect Street....

He went across the hill where Grand Street crosses Broadway, and up past what was then North and is to-day Houston Street, and then turned down a straggling road that ran east and west. He walked toward the Hudson, and passed a farmhouse or two, and came to a bare place where there were no trees, and only a few tangled bushes and ground-vines.

TONY SARG

it." John peeled a fifty dollar bill. The agent, coloring, wished he had asked ten more when he saw John's roll. "We take possession at once. Send me the lease."

"Will you move in today, sir?" He thought them a queer couple, married—perhaps.

"Yes, we'll send over some of our things this afternoon."

"Things, John?" The agent had left. Becka was careful.

"We'll go down on 125th Street and ship out a whole set of furniture; your pick, Becka. Is there anything you want at Mrs. Spector's?"

"Nothing, John, not a thing."

And so they spent the rest of the day, an ecstatic day, purchasing for cash. John stopped off at the bank and drew a thousand dollars. Becka, almost breathless, shrewd, careful, tucked more than half of it away. The new furniture came, bedding, linens, crockery, pans. The things were sent up in an endless number of boxes. The generous city was emptying its riches at their door. John worked, rolled out the two small rugs, helped set up the bed, and Becka, coming in from a near-by grocer's, unloaded a great assortment. The dumb waiter rang. "Meat for Breen!" "Send it up."

In the bathroom the thunder of hot water splashing into the tub, as John washed off the dust and dirt, filled the place with a wholesome activity.

"Me next, John," and when Becka stepped out, in a new pink house gown, her face glowing, her eyes sparkling, John Breen felt like thanking God for the extreme forgiveness that seemed to have come upon him.

"I've got you a half dozen bottles of Piel's dark, John."

W. Parker Chase

New York in 1982 à la Bellamy

from *New York, the Wonder City*
1932

In 1982 New York will likely have so expanded that, if the same ratio of growth in population continues for the coming fifty years as has held for the past fifty, its census will show a community of close to 50,000,000; and its boundary limits including a goodly share of Long Island, as well as absorbing White Plains, Yonkers, and other contiguous territory northward. East River will have been filled in, and hundreds of acres of the Hudson River bed reclaimed.

Buildings will possibly be from 200 to 250 stories in height. Triple-deck elevators, vacuum-tube escalators, and other vertical travel will be so improved as to whisk tenants upwards at a speed surpassing all imagination at this time.

Traffic arrangements will no doubt have provided for several tiers of elevated roadways and noiseless railways—built on extended balconies flanking the enormous skyscrapers, or passing directly through them...so as to keep the streets cleared for *"air-taxi"* ships.

It may be a simple matter for one to eat breakfast in New York and attend the Follies Bergere in Paris that evening. Those who for *some* reason still prefer to *sleep* in Chicago, may be included among New York commuters.

Gilbert Millstein

God and Harvey Grosbeck

1983

The rivers had been obliterated by building. There were vistas of unrelieved tedium and terror. The spires of churches, once the tallest things to be seen in the City, now were no more than gray or brown splinters. The pleasant uniformities of nineteenth-century builders, their private architectural idiosyncrasies, their bits of derivative Greek, or ignorant Renaissance, or Gothic or Baroque, or Beaux Arts, their mingling of a dozen different styles were being pounded into dust, burned, taken away...what had risen on the ashes had no past. The little that was left had been self-consciously prettified into museum exhibits and pointed out to earnest lovers of culture on walking tours....

Varney dictated fluently, mellifluously, with an occasional rounded or chopping motion of the hands. The voice...the voice...the manner. Snake-oil salesman. He could have been standing on the tailgate of a wagon at night, his face lighted by kerosene flares, an audience of appleknockers, mouths open, before him. "...the flagging economy of this great city...a graceful mix of the purely utilitarian and these strong architectural traditions which have made New York what it is...That what you were looking at, Alice?"

"No," she said, "just waiting to hear."

Varney clasped his hands and laid them on the desk. "...incorporating all of what our engineers and designers have learned in the course of a thousand years of discovery...Bernini and Inigo Jones *and* William Le Baron Jenney...you drop in the names, Alice...to produce a city the grandeur of which is unequaled by Rome, Athens or Paris....

"If the City is to be turned around—and such is the strength of our conviction that it can and will be...then—you'll put all this in order, won't you, Miss Forsythe? Inspiration has the habit of showing itself in lumps. I am depending on you to smooth them out—And no one understands more fully than our group the human needs which must be satisfied if the...a domed gallería— Naples? Providence, Rhode Island? You get the idea...walkways paved with the identical blue slate our forebears quarried out of New England hillsides or carried in ballast from the home country to make their rude sidewalks...some reference to Nieuw Amsterdam...the stepped gables of the roofs...THEN...the march of the City through fire, storm, and war, and reconstruction, and so on...Robber Barons...the Fifth Avenue mansions...Custom House...Woolworth Building...the old Waldorf...until we come to this, the perfect jewel carefully fixed in the last waiting bezel in the diadem which will crown this city...the Varney Building..."

"How eloquent, Mr. Varney," said Alice Forsythe, "but what's there now—the mansions—is...well...However, I can understand your enthusiasm."

"Certainly you can, my dear," Varney said, "and I can understand you, but we move on, we put away aimless regrets, we live in our time..."

CHARLES SHEELER

R. O. BLECHMAN

Calvin Trillin
Floater
1980

His musical comedy career came to an end that afternoon. He didn't go back to Nebraska, though. He had, just a week before, found a rent-controlled apartment, and he simply couldn't bear to leave it. Looking for it had, at one point, become virtually a full-time job—rising early to search for the ambulances and police cars that might indicate an opening caused by a fatal heart attack, cultivating sullen West Side elevator men during the lank hours of the afternoon, showing up at Times Square late at night to get a jump on the ads in the early edition of the morning paper—and he was not about to abandon it just as the payoff arrived. The apartment seemed reason enough to remain in the city: for a few months after his watershed confrontation with Syd Berg, he tended to answer the standard cocktail party inquiry "What do you do?" by saying, "I live in a rent-controlled apartment."

Appleton's Dictionary of New York City
1887

Boarding-Houses are the homes of a large number of the permanent as well as transient population of New York, and are of as many grades as there are ranks in society. People living in tenement houses not infrequently "take boarders" in their cramped and dirty apartments, and from this basis boarding-houses rise in size, style, and price to the superb houses in fashionable avenues where every convenience and luxury of a first-class hotel may be obtained. The boarding-houses occupied by the vast army of clerks and salesmen and saleswomen employed on small salaries are all over the city. The rates of board in these houses range from $5 to $10 a week, according to the location of the house and the room occupied. Two meals a day, breakfast and dinner at night, are furnished, and the table is the same for all, variations in price being based solely upon the apartments occupied. Above 8th st. handsome rooms and a good table may be had in almost any street or avenue at prices ranging, for one person, from $10 to $50 a week or more, the price being still graded on the room, so that if two persons occupy one room the price is materially decreased. Strangers or others engaging board would do well to carefully avoid engaging their rooms longer than from week to week, as the presence of disagreeable people or other contingencies frequently make it desirable to change, and an arrangement for a longer term is sure to result in trouble. Americans are exceptionally fond of hotel life, and at all of the hotels there are a large number of permanent boarders, who obtain a concession of from 30 to 50 per cent. from the rates charged to transient guests. Added to the people who live in boarding-houses and hotels, there are many who live in lodgings and take their meals at restaurants and clubs. Particulars in regard to these are given under appropriate headings.

References as to character and responsibility are usually given and required in the better class of boarding-houses; but strangers who are unable to furnish these, if of respectable appearance, are admitted upon payment of their board in advance. In winter an extra charge of 50 cents to $2 a week is made for fires in rooms. Gas is not charged for, nor attendance, but it is well to have all these things stipulated in advance. Many boarding-houses also take lodgers, the taking of meals in the house being optional; this, however, is the exception and not the rule. The general rule in regard to prices is that boarding-houses in 5th av. charge the highest prices, and that these decrease as you go farther east or west; but board on the west side usually costs a little more for the same accommodations than on the east side.

Ernest Poole
The Harbor
1915

One day in the New York office of a big plunger in real estate I pointed to a map on the wall.

"What are all those lots marked 'vacant' for?" I asked him. "I never saw many vacant lots in that part of town." He grinned cheerfully.

"Anything under four stories is vacant to us," he answered, "because it pays to buy it, tear it down and build something higher."...

And I took this front-page view of New York. I saw it as a city where big exceptional people were endlessly doing sensational things, both in the making and spending of money. I saw it not only as a cluster of tall buildings far downtown, but uptown as well a towering pile of rich hotels and apartments, a region that sparkled gaily at night, lights flashing from tens of thousands of rooms, in and out of which, I felt delightedly, millions of people had passed through the years.

Jack Finney
Time and Again
1970

I looked at Kate and she was grinning; then I turned to look south, down the long familiar length of Fifth Avenue, and once more the faintness touched me.

Everyone has seen in actuality or on film the splendid glittering length of Fifth Avenue, the wide wide street solidly lined with incredible towers of metal, glass, and soaring stone: the sparkling Corning Glass Building, its acres of glass walls rising forever; the enormous aluminum-sided Tishman Building; the great stone masses of Rockefeller Center; weather-worn St. Patrick's Cathedral, its twin spires submerged down among the huge buildings which dwarf it. And the sparkling stores: Saks, Tiffany's, Jensen's; and the big, old soiled-white library at the corner of Forty-second Street, its stone lions flanking the wide steps of its main entrance. They must be the most famous seventeen blocks of the world, and beyond them even farther down the length of that astonishing street, the unbelievable height of the Empire State Building at Thirty-fourth Street, if the air should happen to be miraculously clear enough to see it. That was the picture—asphalt and stone and sky-touching towers of metal and glass—that was in my mind instinctively as I turned to look down the length of that street.

Gone. All gone! This street was *tiny!* Narrow! Cobbled! A tree-lined residential street! Mouths open, we stood staring at rows of brownstone houses, at others of brick and stone, at trees, and even patches of fenced snow-covered lawn before the houses. And all down the length of that quiet street, the highest structures I could see were the thin spires of churches, nothing above them but gray winter sky. Coming toward us, rattling on the cobbles of the bare patches of this strange little Fifth Avenue, was another horse-drawn bus, the only moving vehicle, at the moment, in several blocks.

Kate was gripping my arm, whispering. "The Plaza Hotel is gone!" She pointed, and I turned to stare across Fifty-ninth Street to where the Plaza ought to be; instead there was only empty space as though the hotel had been wiped from the scene. We had to stop thinking this way: It hadn't disappeared; it wasn't yet built. But the plaza itself, the little square directly beside Fifth Avenue across the street from the park—it was there, with a fountain at its center, turned off now for the winter. I nudged Kate: "Look. The hack line!" There they stood waiting, the familiar line of half a dozen horse-drawn hacks along the Fifty-ninth Street curb beside the park, where they've been ever since.

We heard the sound, and swung around: The little wooden bus was stopped at the curb beside us, its lantern smudged, and as we walked toward it I caught the sharp stink of oil. The door was at the back, just over a jutting wooden step, and as I opened it for Kate I glanced ahead at the driver, but he was only a motionless, blanket-wrapped figure high on an outside seat at the front, under a heavy umbrella. I followed Kate in, heard reins slap the horses' rumps, the bus jerked forward and we pulled out from the curb. . . .

Inside, two benches ran the short length of the bus under the windows, and Kate sat down beside the rear door while I walked to the tin box up front labeled FARE 5¢. I found two nickels, dropped them in, and noticed the hole in the roof through which the driver could look to see that I did.

And then we sat—there were no other passengers—heads

SEYMOUR CHWAST

swiveling, trying to see both sides of this alien little street at once. Half meaning it, I said, "This isn't Fifth Avenue, it *can't* be," and Kate pointed. Sliding past the window opposite us was a tiny curbside streetlamp, four horizontal strips of painted glass forming a shallow boxlike frame around it, and the painted legend on the panel facing us said 5TH AVENUE.

Kate was pulling my coat sleeve, and when I turned she gestured with her chin at the view behind us. "The Seventies, on the East Side," she said, and I nodded. It was true: The block we were jogging through now looked precisely like some of the tree-lined streets of the East Seventies in modern New York; a row of tall, dignified three- and four-story houses that said *money,* and I knew that different though it seemed this *was* Fifth Avenue. Between Fifty-eighth and Fifty-seventh streets, in fact, on the east side of Fifth, the houses were all of white marble and looked spectacular; and the entire block on the west side of Fifth was filled with a brick-and-gray-stone château.

Philip Hone
Diary of Philip Hone
1835

Everything in New York is at an exorbitant price. Rents have risen fifty per cent. for the next year. I have sold my house, it is true, for a large sum; but where to go I know not. Lots two miles from the City Hall are worth $8,000 or $10,000. Even in the eleventh ward, toward the East river, where they sold two or three years ago for $2,000 or $3,000, they are held now at $4,000 and $5,000. Everything is in the same proportion; the market was higher this morning than I have ever known it,—beef twenty-five cents per pound, mutton and veal fifteen to eighteen cents, small turkeys a dollar and a half. This does very well for persons in business and speculators, who make, as the saying is, "one hand wash another;" but it comes hard upon those retired from business, who live upon fixed incomes, particularly public officers, clerks in banks and counting-houses, whose salaries are never raised in proportion to the increased expense of living.

STOW WENGENROTH

Gay Talese
The Bridge
1964

Montour was a very handsome young man of twenty-six. He had blue eyes, sharp, very un-Indian facial features, almost blond hair. He was married to an extraordinary Indian beauty and had a two-year-old son, and each weekend Danny Montour drove up to the reservation to visit them. He had named his young son after his father, Mark, an ironworker who had crippled himself severely in an automobile accident and had died not long afterward. Danny's paternal grandfather had fallen with the Quebec Bridge in 1907, dying as a result of injuries. His maternal grandfather, also an ironworker, was drunk on the day of the Quebec disaster and, therefore, in no condition to climb the bridge. He later died in an automobile accident.

Despite all this, Danny Montour, as a boy growing up, never doubted that he would become an ironworker. What else would bring such money and position on the reservation? To not become an ironworker was to become a farmer—and to be awakened at 2 A.M. by the automobile horns of returning ironworkers.

So, of the two thousand men on the reservation, few became farmers or clerks or gas pumpers, and fewer became doctors or lawyers, but 1,700 became ironworkers. They could not escape it. It got them when they were babies awakened in their cribs by the horns. The lights would go on, and their mothers would pick them up and bring them downstairs to their fathers, all smiling and full of money and smelling of whiskey or beer, and so happy to be home. They were incapable of enforcing discipline, only capable of handing dollar bills around for the children to play with, and all Indian children grew up with money in their hands. They liked the feel of it, later wanted more of it, *fast*—for fast cars, fast living,

fast trips back and forth between long weekends and endless bridges.

"It's a good life," Danny Montour was trying to explain, driving his car up the Henry Hudson Parkway in New York, past the George Washington Bridge. "You can *see* the job, can see it shape up from a hole in the ground to a tall building or a big bridge."

He paused for a moment, then, looking through the side window at the New York skyline, he said, "You know, I have a name for this town. I don't know if anybody said it before, but I call this town the City of Man-made Mountains. And we're all part of it, and it gives you a good feeling—you're a kind of mountain builder..."

"That's right, Danny-boy, old kid," said Del Stacey, the Indian ironworker who was a little drunk, and sat in the front seat next to Montour with a half-case of beer and bag of ice under his feet. Stacey was a short, plump, copper-skinned young man wearing a straw hat with a red feather in it....

"Sometimes though," Montour continued, "I'd like to stay home more, and see more of my wife and kid..."

"But we can't, Danny-boy," Stacey cut in, cheerfully. "We gotta build them mountains, Danny-boy, and let them women stay home alone, so they'll miss us and won't get a big head, right?" Stacey finished his bottle of beer, then opened a second one with his teeth. The third Indian, in the back seat, was quietly sleeping, having passed out.

NEW BUILDINGS

The turrets leap higher and higher,
　　And the little old homes go down;
The workmen pound on the iron and steel—
　　The woodpeckers of the town.

Charles Hanson Towne
1908

Louis Auchincloss
The Landmarker
from *Tales of Manhattan*
1964

Lefferts' fall was as speedy as social falls always are. He found that he was asked for weekends on Friday night and for dinners on the morning of the party, and soon enough, with the exception of the faithful Bella Hoppin, whose fetish for personal consistency and quasi-royal passion for order fortunately encompassed loyalty to protégés, he was greeted by his old gang with the terrible falsity of the cry: "Chauncey dear! Why do we *never* see you?"

He tried to console himself by saying that society had gone to hell and that he had known, after all, its great days. He tried to consider his years of dining out as a preparation for writing a great novel and played with the idea of becoming a latter-day Proust. He took long walks to recapture the old New York that was dying with him. If he was out-of-date, he was out-of-date like history, out-of-date like the old mansions in which he had dined as a younger man, some of which survived here and there, as boardinghouses or shops, moldering and dowdy, admired only by his faithful self. As time drew on, the façades of these disappearing abodes came to be his sole connection with their former owners, some dead but others merely transplanted and dead now only to him in their distant fashionableness, so that his daily rambles became a sort of social memoir, a retracing in asphalt of his old gay rounds. Living in the past, did people say? Where else *could* he live?

And what a past! He remembered as a young man, before the first war, the exhilaration of riding up Fifth Avenue on the top of an open bus and seeing unfold before him that glorious romp through the Renaissance! He remembered the massive brownstone of the Vanderbilt "twins" at Fifty-first Street, the mellow pink tower of the Gerry château, where the Pierre now stands, and, farther north, the birthday-cake splendor of Senator Clark's and the wide grilled portals of Mrs. Astor that opened to the visitor before he ever touched a bell. And he remembered, too, the long wonderful dinners, to him a peak of civilization, where one arrived happily at eight and departed satisfied at eleven, having spent two of the intervening hours at table over seven courses and five wines.

Oh, people sneered at those parties now, of course. But at least one had known what was expected of one. Today, even at Bella Hoppin's, one never knew how late into the night cocktails might push the battered meal or what ghastly parlor game would be thrust on one afterward. Lefferts lived in a constant secret dread that he would be asked, as a penalty in one of these, to step up on a table and strip before the jeering multitude.

"Well, at least we're *alive*," Bella had once retorted to his protests. "We don't just sit in a row like a herd of dressed-up swine with our noses in the trough. We use our imaginations. I'm afraid you're getting stuffy, Chauncey."

"My idea of heaven," Lefferts muttered, "is a place where one needn't be ashamed to be stuffy."

"Don't turn into a crank, dearie. You haven't the money for that."

Lefferts sighed. It was certainly true that his income, like his invitations, had dropped off. The old grandfather who had limited the modest family trust to railway bonds had ignored the perils of inflation. Had it not been for Bella, who had been his friend since dancing-school days, and a few much younger couples who regarded him beneficently as a social curiosity, rather like a tattered hansom cab parked outside the Plaza, he might have had to dine every night at the Cosmopolitan Club with his maiden sisters who never made even a decent effort to conceal their satisfaction that he should have been dropped at last by Mammon. Poor Lefferts had plenty of opportunity to consider Oscar Wilde's axiom that if to be in society was simply a bore, to be out of it was simply a tragedy.

Happily for him, however, the past did not prove a sterile pursuit. When there were no longer enough houses to visit on his daily walks, he ventured farther afield to seek out other survivals of the great preceding century. In a curious way his need to retreat to it seemed to have a democratizing effect on his attitudes. Anything that shared now in the dignity and grandeur of that greater age—a church, a station, a hotel or a store—shared similarly in his widening affections. He learned the secrets of the rapid transit to be able to visit even the most distant of his new friends, and the same Lefferts who had once walked by the Lady Chapel of St. Patrick's Cathedral and Commodore Farragut's statue in Madison Square without turning his head was now happy to pass a morning traveling underground to the center of Brooklyn for a glimpse of the Gothic gates of Greenwood Cemetery.

It was as if he and the old by-passed city had found each other in a golden twilight. As he stood looking up at Louis Sullivan's terracotta angels with their outstretched arms, high on a cornice over Bleecker Street, or wandered amid the chaste Greek porticos of Snug Harbor, or took in the faded grandeur of Colonnade Row in Lafayette Street, he felt a tremendous upsurge of spirit. This was even more intensely the case when the approach to the landmark was through dingy streets, past yawning warehouses, where Lefferts had to piece his way cautiously and self-consciously, peering ahead until at last he saw, shooting up out of the jumbled masonry, like a nymph rising from her bath, the fine thrust of a Florentine campanile. The very mass of the surrounding city, the engulfing, amorphous, indifferent city, like a huge sow smothering her own offspring, gave to his searches some of the excitement of a consecrating act, as though, a monk in a desperate age, he was solacing his soul by lighting little candles in darkest corners. It even charmed him that the landmarks were frequently merely façades, that the interiors were put to vulgar uses, that bales were stored where there had once been counters of silverware, that dull-eyed lodgers, unconscious of the past and hardly aware of the present, moped in what had once been gilded drawing rooms. The very precariousness of surviving beauty, the mask or shell exposed to a world that never looked up, was analogous to his own threadbare elegance. What was he but a sober, four-story brownstone façade, with Gothic arches and an iron grille, such as one might find in Hicks Street over at Brooklyn Heights?

William Archer
America Today
1899

This is the first sensation of life in New York—you feel that the Americans have practically added a new dimension to space. They move almost as much on the perpendicular as on the horizontal plane. When they find themselves a little crowded, they simply tilt a street on end and call it a skyscraper.

Theodore Dreiser
The Color of a Great City
1923

I once knew a poor, half-demented, and very much shriveled little seamstress who occupied a tiny hall-bedroom in a side-street rooming-house, cooked her meals on a small alcohol stove set on a bureau, and who had about space enough outside of this to take three good steps either way.

"I would rather live in my hall-bedroom in New York than in any fifteen-room house in the country that I ever saw," she commented once, and her poor little colorless eyes held more of sparkle and snap in them than I ever saw there, before or after.

Stephen Graham
New York Nights
1927

Shaw in *Pygmalion* identified the suburban habitats of people in a crowd by the characteristic differences in their cockney accent. In New York a clever reader of faces might be able to tell at a glance on what floor a man lived. People are beginning to get a 15th floor look. Faces of mountaineers are beginning to appear in the streets of New York, uplifted, bardic. There is a great deal of difference between the depressed expressions of those who dwell on ground-floors and those who inhabit the peaks. It is a terrible burden to carry the sense of there being twenty storeys above one. The pioneers of Manhattan are up in the cerulean; these are the people with the views and the air; the people who have got out of the shadow. They go to the window and say, "Just look out at this marvellous wonderful city." Those living down below are denied these views and get a cellar expression on their faces.

"If you're passing just drop up," says a friend to me. In what other city in the world could one hear such an expression?

A. MAXWELL FRY

A. MAXWELL FRY

F. Scott Fitzgerald
City Dwellers
from My *Lost City*
1932

The city was bloated, glutted, stupid with cake and circuses, and a new expression "Oh yeah?" summed up all the enthusiasm evoked by the announcement of the last super-skyscrapers.

Helen Keller
A Romantic Edifice
1929

Standing there 'twixt earth and sky, I saw a romantic edifice wrought by human brains and hands that is to the burning eye of the sun a rival luminary. I saw it stand erect and serene in the midst of storm and tumult of elemental commotion. I heard the hammer of Thor ring when the shaft began to rise upward. I saw the unconquerable steel, the flash of testing flames, the sword-like rivets. I heard the steel drills in pandemonium. I saw countless skilled workers welding together that mighty symmetry. I looked upon the marvel of frail yet indomitable hands that lifted the tower to its dominating height.

W. S. L. JEWETT

Theodore Dreiser

Sister Carrie

1900

Whatever a man like Hurstwood could be in Chicago, it is very evident that he would be but an inconspicuous drop in an ocean like New York. In Chicago, whose population still ranged about 500,000, millionaires were not numerous. The rich had not become so conspicuously rich as to drown all moderate incomes in obscurity. The attention of the inhabitants was not so distracted by local celebrities in the dramatic, artistic, social, and religious fields as to shut the well-positioned man from view. In Chicago the two roads to distinction were politics and trade. In New York the roads were any one of a half-hundred, and each had been diligently pursued by hundreds, so that celebrities were numerous. The sea was already full of whales. A common fish must needs disappear wholly from view—remain unseen. In other words, Hurstwood was nothing.

Mark Twain

John Chinaman in New York

1870

As I passed along by one of those monster American tea stores in New York, I found a Chinaman sitting before it acting in the capacity of a sign. Everybody that passed by gave him a steady stare as long as their heads would twist over their shoulders without dislocating their necks, and a group had stopped to stare deliberately.

Is it not a shame that we, who prate so much about civilization and humanity, are content to degrade a fellow-being to such an office as this? Is it not time for reflection when we find ourselves willing to see in such a being matter for frivolous curiosity instead of regret and grave reflection? Here was a poor creature whom hard fortune had exiled from his natural home beyond the seas, and whose troubles ought to have touched these idle strangers that thronged about him; but did it? Apparently not. Men calling themselves the superior race, the race of culture and of gentle blood, scanned his quaint Chinese hat, with peaked roof and ball on top, and his long queue dangling down his back; his short silken blouse, curiously frogged and figured (and, like the rest of his raiment, rusty, dilapidated, and awkwardly put on); his blue cotton, tight-legged pants, tied close around the ankles; and his clumsy blunt-toed shoes with thick cork soles; and having so scanned him from head to foot, cracked some unseemly joke about his outlandish attire or his melancholy face, and passed on. In my heart I pitied the friendless Mongol. I wondered what was passing

behind his sad face, and what distant scene his vacant eye was dreaming of. Were his thoughts with his heart, ten thousand miles away, beyond the billowy wastes of the Pacific? among the ricefields and the plumy palms of China? under the shadows of remembered mountain peaks, or in groves of bloomy shrubs and strange forest trees unknown to climes like ours? And now and then, rippling among his visions and his dreams, did he hear familiar laughter and half-forgotten voices, and did he catch fitful glimpses of the friendly faces of a bygone time? A cruel fate it is, I said, that is befallen this bronzed wanderer. In order that the group of idlers might be touched at least by the words of the poor fellow, since the appeal of his pauper dress and his dreary exile was lost upon them, I touched him on the shoulder and said:

"Cheer up—don't be downhearted. It is not America that treats you in this way, it is merely one citizen, whose greed of gain has eaten the humanity out of his heart. America has a broader hospitality for the exiled and oppressed. America and Americans are always ready to help the unfortunate. Money shall be raised—you shall go back to China—you shall see your friends again. What wages do they pay you here?"

"Divil a cint but four dollars a week and find meself; but it's aisy, barrin' the troublesome furrin clothes that's so expinsive."

The exile remains at his post. The New York tea merchants who need picturesque signs are not likely to run out of Chinamen.

C. BUNNELL

THOMAS NAST

William Riordan

Tammany Leaders Not Bookworms

from *Plunkitt of Tammany Hall*
1905

You hear a lot of talk about the Tammany district leaders bein' illiterate men. If illiterate means havin' common sense, we plead guilty. But if they mean that the Tammany leaders ain't got no education and ain't gents they don't know what they're talkin' about. Of course, we ain't all bookworms and college professors. If we were, Tammany might win an election once in four thousand years. Most of the leaders are plain American citizens, of the people and near to the people, and they have all the education they need to whip the dudes who part their name in the middle and to run the City Government. We've got bookworms, too, in the organization. But we don't make them district leaders. We keep them for ornaments on parade days.

Tammany Hall is a great big machine, with every part adjusted delicate to do its own particular work. It runs so smooth that you wouldn't think it was a complicated affair, but it is. Every district leader is fitted to the district he runs and he wouldn't exactly fit any other district. That's the reason Tammany never makes the mistake the Fusion outfit always makes of sendin' men into the districts who don't know the people, and have no sympathy with their peculiarities. We don't put a silk stockin' on the Bowery, nor do we make a man who is handy with his fists leader of the Twenty-ninth. The Fusionists make about the same sort of a mistake that a repeater made at an election in Albany several years ago. He was hired to go to the polls early in a half-dozen election districts and vote on other men's names before these men reached the polls. At one place, when he was asked his name by the poll clerk, he had the nerve to answer "William Croswell Doane."

"Come off. You ain't Bishop Doane," said the poll clerk.

"The hell I ain't, you————!" yelled the repeater.

Now, that is the sort of bad judgment the Fusionists are guilty of. They don't pick men to suit the work they have to do.

Take me, for instance. My district, the Fifteenth, is made up of all sorts of people, and a cosmopolitan is needed to run it successful. I'm a cosmopolitan. When I get into the silk-stockin' part of the district, I can talk grammar and all that with the best of them. I went to school three winters when I was a boy, and I learned a lot of fancy stuff that I keep for occasions. There ain't a silk stockin' in the district who ain't proud to be seen talkin' with George Washington Plunkitt, and maybe they learn a thing or two from their talks with me. There's one man in the district, a big banker, who said to me one day: "George, you can sling the most vigorous English I ever heard. You remind me of Senator Hoar of Massachusetts." Of course, that was puttin' it on too thick; but say, honest, I like Senator Hoar's speeches. He once quoted in the United States Senate some of my remarks on the curse of civil service, and, though he didn't agree with me altogether, I noticed that our ideas are alike in some things, and we both have the knack of puttin' things strong, only he put on more frills to suit his audience. . . .

A cosmopolitan ain't needed in all the other districts, but our men are just the kind to rule. There's Dan Finn, in the Battery district, bluff, jolly Dan, who is now on the bench. Maybe you'd think that a court justice is not the man to hold a district like that, but you're mistaken. Most of the voters of the district are the janitors of the big office buildings on lower Broadway and their helpers. These janitors are the most dignified and haughtiest of men. Even I would have trouble in holding them. Nothin' less than a judge on the bench is good enough for them. Dan does the dignity act with the janitors, and when he is with the boys he hangs up the ermine in the closet and becomes a jolly good fellow.

Charles Dickens
American Notes
1842

Was there ever such a sunny street as this Broadway! The pavement stones are polished with the tread of feet until they shine again; the red bricks of the houses might be yet in the dry, hot kilns; and the roofs of those omnibuses look as though, if water were poured on them, they would hiss and smoke, and smell like half-quenched fires. No stint of omnibuses here! Half-a-dozen have gone by within as many minutes. Plenty of hackney cabs and coaches too; gigs, phaetons, large-wheeled tilburies, and private carriages—rather of a clumsy make, and not very different from the public vehicles, but built for the heavy roads beyond the city pavement. Negro coachmen and white; in straw hats, black hats, white hats, glazed caps, fur caps; in coats of drab, black, brown, green, blue, nankeen, striped jean and linen; and there, in that one instance (look while it passes, or it will be too late), in suits of livery. Some southern republican that, who puts his blacks in uniform, and swells with Sultan pomp and power. Yonder, where that phaeton with the well-clipped pair of grays has stopped . . . is a Yorkshire groom, who has not been very long in these parts, and looks sorrowfully round for a companion pair of top-boots, which he may traverse the city half a year without meeting. Heaven save the ladies, how they dress! We have seen more colours in these ten minutes, than we should have seen elsewhere, in as many days. What various parasols! what rainbow silks and satins! what pinking of thin stockings, and pinching of thin shoes, and fluttering of ribbons and silk tassels, and display of rich cloaks with gaudy hoods and linings! The young gentlemen are fond, you see, of turning down their shirt-collars and cultivating their whiskers, especially under the chin; but they cannot approach the ladies in their dress or bearing, being, to say the truth, humanity of quite another sort. . . .

Again across Broadway, and so—passing from the many-coloured crowd and glittering shops—into another long main street, the Bowery. A railroad yonder, see, where two stout horses trot along, drawing a score or two of people and a great wooden ark, with ease. The stores are poorer here; the passengers less gay. Clothes ready-made, and meat ready-cooked, are to be bought in these parts; and the lively whirl of carriages is exchanged for the deep rumble of carts and wagons. These signs which are so plentiful, in shape like river buoys, or small balloons, hoisted by cords to poles, and dangling there, announce, as you may see by looking up, 'OYSTERS IN EVERY STYLE.' They tempt the hungry most at night, for then dull candles glimmering inside, illuminate these dainty words, and make the mouths of idlers water, as they read and linger.

John Sloan
John Sloan's New York
1965

March 21 [1907] A letter from Walter Norris in his own print of hand—says he has had a narrow squeak but is gaining weight. I hope that his recovery is assured. A very beautiful day with a strong touch of Spring. I walked down Broadway to Union Square. Got proofs from "Everybody's" which are quite unsatisfactory to me. The engravers have made "rush" halftones. Worked on a Puzzle, finished it in evening. Henri came in to dinner. . . . There is a fine appreciation of George Luks in the Sun this morning. A beautiful example of Huneker's ability to interest in art criticism. Though appreciation is what he does he's different from the average critic in that they usually think that they are sent by God to shield mankind from what they don't care for themselves.

March 22 Mrs. Montgomery arrived today to stay over night. Nell and I crossed the ferry and met her and after lunch Dolly and Nell and she went out to see the town . . . painted in the afternoon on "The Wake of the Ferry." In the evening, Mrs. M. treated us to a trip to the Hippodrome. A huge playhouse and a spectacular show. Am puzzled as to how they manage to have people rise up from the water in the big stage tank. A storm off the coast of France is a big piece of stage effect. After show we went to Churchill's restaurant and saw the Gay Ones of Broadway.

March 23 We all started down to the Aquarium at the Battery and then came up by subway to Café Francis and had lunch. Met Lawson, Glackens, Preston, Fangel and the girls left and I stayed the afternoon which was very agreeable—reminiscences of the Philadelphia "Press" days. . . . Home at 6:30 P.M. Mr. Montgomery came from Phila. and we all went to "Maria's" for dinner. Then to the Chinese quarter, Bowery, and Pell Street where our visitors were very much interested in the streets and shops. We ate in a restaurant, gorgeous in teakwood carving, mother of pearl, gold and rough customers.

March 24 Today to the Metropolitan Museum of Art. My first visit for a long time. Rather dreary—there was little enough to interest me and very little to our company—and galleries are tiring at their best. We rode down in the Fifth Avenue Bus displaying the houses of the rich to our Philadelphians with a sense of pride (as though we were entitled to the credit). To the Francis where we had lunch. Then the Montgomerys left by the 5 o'clock train and Dolly, Nell and I went by ferry to Weehawken. Dined at Reuterdahl's. Met a Swedish author, a name that sounded like "Wrangel" who is writing a series of essays on the U.S. Benson was there and it was a good dinner....

March 25 Dropped in to Macbeth's Gallery and among other things saw a Luks picture, mare and foal, wagon at brow of hill. A fine Spring day. Fifth Avenue looked fine. Murray Hill is a fine sight up or down. Sat in Madison Square and watched the children at play. Two young nurse girls playing ball, watched by bums, self and others—varying reasons.... I started on a memory of the paths of Madison Square. Evening at home. A letter from Connah of N.Y. School of Art Gallery asks for pictures for an exhibition of the work of the "crowd" which I am doubtful about. Seems to me that it would not have sufficient importance and yet perhaps every chance should be taken to exhibit the work.

March 26 Walked out to lay in supplies in the liquid refreshment line. Loafed in Madison Square a while. Painted in the afternoon.... Henri, J. B. Moore, F. J. Gregg to dinner which Dolly prepared in elegant style. Henri showed proofs of G. O. Coleman's drawings in portfolio. Very good things, $3.00 a set. I ordered one, so did Gregg and J. Moore....

September 15 Walked out for papers. The leaves in Madison Square are commencing to show the touch of fall, very beautiful rich color and the brass trimmings of the automobiles dashing by on Fifth Avenue suggest a picture to me. The brass of the life of those riding. Finished the Sunday Magazine Bull Fight drawings....

April 19 [1908] A raw, blustery day with a shower now and then, but with a beautiful sky, huge cloud masses. At 4:30 in the afternoon, Dolly and I started to the 23rd St. ferry to go to Mrs. Crane's father's home in Hoboken... a wonderful sky breaking open in the West, heavy-laden blue clouds and south above the horizon a strip of gray-orange. Against this the huge Mauretania silhouetted with vermilion stacks and black hull. I think I have never seen a day that made the city and the works of man so beautiful.... Dolly and I came home by the new "tube" under the Hudson, quite a novel sensation. Smells like a damp cellar. We came from Hoboken to 19th and Sixth Ave. in about fifteen minutes.

Stephen Crane
A Detail
from *Midnight Sketches*
1896

The tiny old lady in the black dress and curious little black bonnet had at first seemed alarmed at the sound made by her feet upon the stone pavements. But later she forgot about it, for she suddenly came into the tempest of the Sixth Avenue shopping district, where from the streams of people and vehicles went up a roar like that from headlong mountain torrents.

She seemed then like a chip that catches, recoils, turns, and wheels, a reluctant thing in the clutch of the impetuous river. She hesitated, faltered.... Frequently she seemed about to address people; then of a sudden she would evidently lose her courage. Meanwhile the torrent jostled her, swung her this and that way.

At last, however, she saw two young women gazing in at a shop window. They were well-dressed girls; they wore gowns with enormous sleeves that made them look like full-rigged ships with all sails set. They seemed to have plenty of time; they leisurely scanned the goods in the window. Other people had made the tiny old woman much afraid because obviously they were speeding to keep such tremendously important engagements. She went close to the girls and peered in at the same window. She watched them furtively for a time. Then finally she said: "Excuse me!"

The girls looked down at this old face with its two large eyes turned toward them.

"Excuse me: can you tell me where I can get any work?"

For an instant the two girls stared. Then they seemed about to exchange a smile, but, at the last moment, they checked it. The tiny old lady's eyes were upon them. She was quaintly serious, silently expectant. She made one marvel that in that face the wrinkles showed no trace of experience, knowledge; they were simply little soft, innocent creases. As for her glance, it had the trustfulness of ignorance and the candor of babyhood.

"I want to get something to do, because I need the money," she continued, since, in their astonishment, they had not replied to her first question. "Of course I'm not strong and I couldn't do very much, but I can sew well; and in a house where there was a good many menfolks, I could do all the mending. Do you know any place where they would like me to come?"

The young women did then exchange a smile, but it was a subtle tender smile, the edge of personal grief.

"Well, no, madam," hesitatingly said one of them at last; "I don't think I know any one."

A shade passed over the tiny old lady's face, a shadow of the wing of disappointment. "Don't you?" she said, with a little struggle to be brave in her voice.

Then the girl hastily continued: "But if you will give me your address, I may find some one, and if I do, I will surely let you know of it."

The tiny old lady dictated her address, bending over to watch the girl write on a visiting card with a little silver pencil. Then she said: "I thank you very much." She bowed to them, smiling, and went on down the avenue.

As for the two girls, they walked to the curb and watched this aged figure, small and frail, in its black gown and curious black bonnet. At last, the crowd, the innumerable wagons, intermingling and changing with uproar and riot, suddenly engulfed it.

Anonymous

Prostitution Exposed

Or, A Moral Reform Directory
1839

Mother Miller.

In Reed-street, No. 133, a few doors from Hudson St., stands a three story brick house, of respectable appearance; this is occupied by Mrs. Miller, an elderly Cyprian, of about sixty years of age, and about thirteen girls, generally of good appearance and address. She usually dresses in black, with a plaid handkerchief tied round her head to conceal her grey hairs from view. The history of this woman is somewhat singular. She has buried three husbands, two of which she has had children by. Miss Josephine Clifton, now a prominent star in our Theatres, is one of her daughters, and Miss Missouri Miller, who died so mysteriously while under the guardianship of Hamblin, is another child of "Old Jezabel;" she has other children whom it is needless to mention their names. To each of her daughters she gave elegant and classic educations, and kept them free from the lazaar house of crime. To this old Courtezan's credit be it said, she has exerted herself to bring her daughters up respectably, and it is believed succeeded. Mother Miller's worst fault is avarice; to this may be attributed her present situation, as the keeper of a house of ill-fame. After the death of her last husband, who left her in possession of a large property, her attorney persuaded her to let her buildings for houses of prostitution which she consented to, and finding her tenants able to pay such large rents, she concluded she would embark in the same profession, in which she still continues. She is estimated to be worth $100,000. This being a house of the first class, the price of lodging varies from $10 to $25, according to customer. Champaigne $3. Breakfast Free.

Jane P. Williams,

Resides at 148 Leonard street, near Orange. Rather well-favored, and about 35 years of age. Keeps a good house, and some very handsome girls. Prices moderate.

Rachel Fields,

A beautiful courtezan, is kept by one of the Bowery black-legs at a house in Howard-st. near Broadway. First seduction not known. She is used by her paramour to swear him out of difficulty when arrested for crime.

Ellen Jewell,

No. 55 Leonard-street, is a splendid dashy woman, and keeps the loudest kind of a house—only 6 girls.

FIFTH EDITION—WITH MANY ADDITIONS.

PROSTITUTION EXPOSED;

OR, A

MORAL REFORM DIRECTORY,

LAYING BARE THE

Lives, Histories, Residences, Seductions, &c.

OF THE MOST CELEBRATED

COURTEZANS AND LADIES OF PLEASURE

OF THE CITY OF NEW-YORK,

Together with a Description of the Crime and its Effects,

AS ALSO, OF THE

Houses of Prostitution and their Keepers,

HOUSES OF ASSIGNATION,

THEIR CHARGES AND CONVENIENCES,

AND OTHER PARTICULARS INTERESTING TO THE PUBLIC.

BY A BUTT ENDER.

NEW-YORK:

PUBLISHED FOR PUBLIC CONVENIENCE.

1839.

Elizabeth Ingersoll,

A small, fair complected girl, about twenty-three years old, promenades Broadway and Mercer-streets, and escorts her company to Ann Burt's in Orange-street. A regular fire-ship. Is the well known chum of the celebrated blazing slut called the "*Great Western*," who is a noted street thrumper.

Moll Steele,

Resides two doors west of West Broadway, and keeps a house of the middling class. Charges from two to five dollars. She has five rather handsome damsels under her matronly care.

Mrs. Bush,

Resides in Scammel-street, in a yellow house, next door to the All-Saint's Church. Formerly the kept-mistress of a sloop-captain, who is a married man, and whose wife occasionally has caught him at the house of his dulcina. Her daughter, who resides with her, a beautiful little girl of 15, has had an illegitimate child by a certain flash-cove well known in that neighborhood.

Mrs. Quinn,

Resides in a three-story wooden building, No 102 Division-street, is a small statured, red-haired hussey, and a common affair. There are two others who live in the rear building, too common to describe.

Becky Wayman,

Keeps a splendid establishment, 62 Mott-street, well known to the Bowery and Grand-street Dry Goods merchants and their clerks. It is not an uncommon thing for one of the former to meet his clerk at this house, indulging himself at the expense of his employers till. It is a large yellow house, and very orderly and quiet in the interior.

Mrs. Brown,

Resides in Goerck-st. opposite the Corporation Yard. All the boys of that neighborhood shun her, not being desirous of too close an intimacy.

Lucy Raydon,

Alias, half a dozen other names, lives in a splendid nunnery, a few doors from Grand, in Wooster, next door to a carriage Repository. She is considered as top of the heap.

Mary Benson,

Lives at Julia Brown's, 100 Church-street, and is a nun of the most rigid order; she is constantly subject to the attacks of the male visitors of that house, because she will not violate her *chastity* for less than a V.

Cordelia Watson,

Lives at Mother Smith's in Centre-street. She is rather good looking, and about 21 years of age. Has been in the public line four years.

Abby Mead,

Alias Abby Myers, 134 Duane-street. The interior of this establishment is better arranged than any other in the city. There are two parlors separated by folding doors; the front apartment is kept dark, and is occupied by ladies who are not and cannot be seen, as they are generally composed of married and unmarried females who are not tenants of the house, but visit it to obtain a portion of carnal pleasure; the room is kept dark so that they may not be recognized even by their companions for the night. The other parlor is lighted and is the resort of those more barefaced. This house is decidedly A. No. 1, for respectability. The proprietor, Mrs. M. lives principally at her country seat on Long Island.

Margaret Van Tassel.

A tall, exquisitely formed, splendid woman, keeps a house at No. 6 Franklin-St., formerly occupied for the same business by Susan Byron, as also by Mrs. Moore. First seduced by a Circus Rider, and afterwards kept by a preparer of Artist's colors. Girls of surpassing beauty.

Mrs. Sweet,

Proprietor of 24 Wooster-street, resides at a private domicil in the upper part of the city, and leaves her business to an agency. A first rate house. . . .

Lucinda Pease,

A full slushy piece who has passed through every degree of prostitution, from the kept mistress to the lowest *blazer*, and been sentenced and confined in the penitentiary for prostitution, resides in Mangin-street, three doors from Broome. Young men must be cautious of her company. She lately became religious, but is at present a *backslider*.

Don Freeman

Apple Annie

from *Come One Come All*
1949

Apple Annie sold apples even before the depression. She held down her stand under the fire escape outside the Astor Theater on 45th Street just off Broadway. On my way to and from the theaters I had never given her more than a passing glance. She seemed like some character from a play as she sat there on a bench in her thin coat and faded hat, her feet in their worn shoes resting on a few layers of newspaper to keep away the chill of the sidewalks.

On one especially cold day, after having passed her by hundreds of times before along with the rest of the hurrying crowds, I couldn't resist buying one of her shiny red apples.

"No, business isn't so very good these days," she said, in such a way that I suspected she forgave everyone for running past her.

To hear her speak and to look into her eyes was assurance enough that she was not merely filling a niche under a fire escape

CLARE LEIGHTON

to help give Broadway its local color. It was imperative that she sell her apples. After this first visit with her I stopped regularly and we soon became good friends.

Her husband Tom had once been a shoe salesman and now sold shoelaces down in the Wall Street section. One evening as he called for his Annie, I had the honor of meeting him. He was of the same meek who shall inherit the earth—that is, if they can hold out long enough. Both he and his wife maintained a serene dignity seemingly untouched by Broadway.

On the brick wall behind Apple Annie's stand were pasted some wind-torn and faded clippings from various New York newspapers. They were news reports describing the biggest day in her life, the time she was feted and fussed over as part of a publicity stunt for the opening of a movie. She had been whisked around in a limousine to the Waldorf-Astoria and given a suite of rooms, taken to a beauty parlor and dressed in a fancy dress, just for a day.

It was a sad affair for her to remember, if the truth were known, but few people knew the facts. Annie was not one to tell her troubles to everybody she met. What made her feel most unhappy was the fact that certain newspapers had reported that she received a large amount of money for her part in the publicity stunt. This made her friends along the stem, those who sold flowers, gum and newspapers, believe she had earned a lot of money.

"All I ever got was twenty-five dollars," Apple Annie confided, "but everybody thinks I'm a wealthy woman now. I was made a fool of for a day, that's what I was."

The one friend on the street who knew more than anyone else how badly Annie felt was Sam, the shoeshiner. He kept his box just a short distance down the block. He knew that when Annie was not at her stand for two weeks after the publicity stunt, it was probably because she became ill from the ordeal and not because she was "too stuckup" to sell apples any more.

"But when she came back, nobody paid her no mind no more," Sam said.

Just before matinee time, when I stopped to see Apple Annie on a bitter cold November afternoon, she asked me if I would mind taking her place at the stand while she went across the street to the Astor Drug Store for coffee. I sat down on the small bench and during those next few minutes I found out what real misery was like. The bricks behind me held the cold like a wall of ice and I was nearly frozen by the time Annie returned. When people walked by without buying the bright apples I began to feel their icy unconcern and callous indifference. My only sale was to a chauffeur who parked a limousine outside a theater, and he eyed me with suspicion.

For weeks I had been wanting to make a painting of Apple Annie and now, when I visualized her sitting beside the radiator in my room, my conscience felt somewhat soothed. She seemed happy over the idea and I asked when she could come. She named the following Thursday as the day to pick her up.

The sun came out on that Thursday and everyone welcomed its unexpected break-through. Knowing who would be the happiest person in the world to see the sun, I whistled along with the rest of the crowd down Broadway. But when I came to 45th Street there was not a sign of Apple Annie at her usual place under the fire escape.

Sam, the shoeshiner near by, said no, he hadn't seen her all that day or the day before either. This was certainly strange since she had scarcely ever missed a day. On Saturday I went up again but she was still not there.

When Sam saw me, he came over holding a folded newspaper. As he handed me the paper he pointed to a small item at the bottom of the back page. It reported that Mr. and Mrs. Tom McCarthy had died in their sleep from gas fumes from a faulty range in their furnished room at 203 Eighth Avenue. The report ended by stating that Mrs. McCarthy was well known along Broadway as Apple Annie.

The once-exuberant song of the city suddenly modulated into a minor key. Through the frivolous exterior of its gay, swarming crowds I began seeing the cruel gray reality that lay everywhere underneath.

But Broadway as usual lit up like a giant birthday cake and no one seemed to care about or notice the absent apple stand under the fire escape on West 45th Street.

Damon Runyon
Cafe Society
from *My Wife Ethel*
1939

Brooklyn, June 6.

DEAR SIR last week I got a raise in salary and when I went home and told my wife Ethel she ses why Joe that is wonderful. Now you can take me stepping to celebrate it.

I ses all right baby where do you want to go? She ses Joe I want to go over to the Stork Club and see the cafe society. I ses what is the cafe society? Ethel ses well it is the society that you see in places like the Stork Club. I have been reading about it in the papers and it must be wonderful.

I ses well Ethel honey nothing is too good for a winner. I ses I will take you to the Stork Club and you can see all the cafe society you want. So I put on my tux and she put on her new evening dress and we went to the Stork Club and had dinner and knocked off a couple of rhumbas and I ses to Ethel where is the cafe society?

She ses why Joe all these people here eating and drinking and dancing are the cafe society. I ses well they look like anybody else to me. I ses they do not look any different to me than the people I see at Grogans over in Flatbush Avenue. Ethel ses O Joe you are wrong. They are much different. You can see they are a lot classier than the people you find in Grogans and I am surprised you do not notice it.

I ses what is classier about them? Ethel ses well it is the way they look. I only wish I knew some of their names. I bet anything they are the very same names I read in the papers. I ses well Ethel I see a waiter over in the corner that used to work in Grogans. I ses if you like I will call him over and maybe he will tell us who somebody is. I ses his name is Pietro and he is a nice fellow. Ethel ses now Joe Turp don't you be talking to waiters like they was old friends of yours the way you always do. What would the cafe society think of us? I ses well he is an old friend of mine and what do I care what anybody thinks? Ethel ses well I do so never mind that waiter. Joe do you think anybody has noticed my new dress?

I ses baby there is not so much of your dress for them to notice but I bet they have noticed that. Ethel ses noticed what? I ses noticed that there is not so much of it to notice. She ses I do not know what you mean. This dress cost sixteen ninety-five and it is the latest thing. I think those ladies at that table over in the corner noticed it. I ses well baby anybody that did not notice that dress and what is in it must be blind. I ses now you just set here a minute while I go brush my hair and then we will show these chumps some more about dancing.

ISAC FRIEDLANDER

Upton Sinclair
The Metropolis
1907

Montague had come to begin life all over again. He had brought his money, and he expected to invest it, and to live upon the income until he had begun to earn something. He had worked hard at his profession, and he meant to work in New York, and to win his way in the end. He knew almost nothing about the city— he faced it with the wide-open eyes of a child.

One began to learn quickly, he found. It was like being swept into a maelstrom: first the hurrying throngs on the ferry-boat, and then the cabmen and newsboys shouting, and the cars with clanging gongs; then the swift motor, gliding between trucks and carriages and around corners where big policemen shepherded the scurrying populace; and then Fifth Avenue, with its rows of shops and towering hotels; and at last a sudden swing round a corner— and their home.

"I have picked a quiet family place for you," Oliver had said, and that had greatly pleased his brother. But he had stared in dismay when he entered this latest "apartment hotel"—which catered to two or three hundred of the most exclusive of the city's aristocracy—and noted its great arcade, with massive doors of bronze, and its entrance-hall, trimmed with Caen stone and Italian marble, and roofed with a vaulted ceiling painted by modern masters. Men in livery bore their wraps and bowed the way before them; a great bronze elevator shot them to the proper floor; and they went to their rooms down a corridor walled with blood-red marble and paved with carpet soft as a cushion. Here were six rooms of palatial size, with carpets, drapery, and furniture of a splendor quite appalling to Montague.

As soon as the man who bore their wraps had left the room, he turned upon his brother.

"Oliver," he said, "how much are we paying for all this?"

Oliver smiled. "You are not paying anything, old man," he replied. "You're to be my guests for a month or two, until you get your bearings."

"That's very good of you," said the other; "—we'll talk about it later. But meantime, tell me what the apartment costs."

And then Montague encountered his first full charge of New York dynamite. "Six hundred dollars a week," said Oliver.

He started as if his brother had struck him. "Six hundred dollars a week!" he gasped.

"Yes," said the other, quietly.

It was fully a minute before he could find his breath. "Brother," he exclaimed, "you're mad!"

"It is a very good bargain," smiled the other; "I have some influence with them."

Again there was a pause, while Montague groped for words. "Oliver," he exclaimed, "I can't believe you! How could you think that we could pay such a price?"

"I didn't think it," said Oliver; "I told you I expected to pay it myself."

"But how could we let you pay it for us?" cried the other. "Can you fancy that *I* will ever earn enough to pay such a price?"

"Of course you will," said Oliver. "Don't be foolish, Allan— you'll find it's easy enough to make money in New York. Leave it to me, and wait awhile."

But the other was not to be put off. He sat down on the embroidered silk bedspread, and demanded abruptly, "What do you expect my income to be a year?"

"I'm sure I don't know," laughed Oliver; "nobody takes the time to add up his income. You'll make what you need, and something over for good measure. This one thing you'll know for certain—the more you spend, the more you'll be able to make."

And then, seeing that the sober look was not to be expelled from his brother's face, Oliver seated himself and crossed his legs, and proceeded to set forth the paradoxical philosophy of extravagance. His brother had come into a city of millionaires. There was a certain group of people—"the right set," was Oliver's term for them—and among them he would find that money was as free as air. So far as his career was concerned, he would find that there was nothing in all New York so costly as economy. If he did not live like a gentleman, he would find himself excluded from the circle of the elect—and how he would manage to exist then was a problem too difficult for his brother to face.

Henry Miller
The Ghetto

from *Sexus*
1949

A man of an olden race standing in a stone trance. He smells the food which his ancestors cooked in the millenary past: the chicken, the liver paste, the stuffed fish, the herrings, the eiderdown ducks. He has lived with them and they have lived in him. Feathers float through the air, the feathers of winged creatures caged in crates—as it was in Ur, in Babylon, in Egypt and Palestine. The same shiny silks, blacks turning green with age: the silks of other times, of other cities, other ghettos, other pogroms. Now and then a coffee grinder or a samovar, a little wooden casket for spices, for the myrrh and aloes of the East. Little strips of carpet—from the souks and bazaars, from the emporiums of the Levant; bits of astrakhan, laces, shawls, nubies, and petticoats of flaming, flouncing flamingo. Some bring their birds, their little pets—warm, tender things pulsing with tremulous beat, learning no new language, no new melodies, but pining away, droopy, listless, languishing in their super-heated cages suspended above the fire escapes. The iron balconies are festooned with meat and bedding, with plants and pets—a crawling still life in which even the rust is rapturously eaten away. With the cool of the evening the young are exposed like eggplants; they lie back under the stars, lulled to dream by the obscene jabberwocky of the American street. Below, in wooden casks, are the pickles floating in brine. Without the pickle, the pretzel, the Turkish sweets, the ghetto would be without savor. Bread of every variety, with seeds and without. White, black, brown, even gray bread—of all weights, all consistencies. . . .

EVE CHWAST

Theodore L. Kazimiroff
A Strange Meeting

from *The Last Algonquin*
1982

When I was a boy in 1924, began my father, I used to walk from my house in Throggs Neck to the woody hills of Hunter and Twin Islands as often as I could. That area fascinated me because it contained almost all the flora and fauna that I had read about in my Boy Scout manuals. I found both glacial boulders and scratches, evidence of the great ice sheet that had descended on the Bronx from the North. I picked and ate berries and fruits of varieties my mother never saw in stores. The rocky shores provided me with ample specimens for my geology studies. Fresh water ran from several springs on the islands, and so I could be self-sufficient for a day, without even bringing along a lunch or canteen. There was no Orchard Beach here yet to attract people in any number, and often I could spend an entire day walking field and shore without seeing another person. I had no idea then that the reverse was seldom true. When a bush would quiver without a breeze to prod it, I would dismiss it as a small animal frightened by my intrusion into this solitude. For many months I was quite unaware that I was being watched.

Then one day I discovered a rabbit run in the underbrush. It was heavily tamped down indicating the passage of many little feet. I decided to follow it and see if I could stalk up to a cottontail and touch him. I had touched a deer that way once at the Boy Scout camp upstate.

For a while it was easy going as I followed through the low brush, but as I went along it became heavier. Soon I was on all fours, crawling under blackberry brambles and thick bushes. A few feet ahead, a cut branch caught my eye and I went over to take a closer look. The cut wood was all that showed of a very ingenious noose-snare, made entirely of wood and bark strips. During the following months, alerted by the snare I had found, I quietly noticed other signs of possible habitation in my woodland retreat. The possibility that someone could live here, unobserved by even so regular a visitor as myself, was intriguing. I continued my observation through the summer and into the early fall. I was studying the animal life and the botanical and geological portions in preparation for several merit badges I wanted for my scouting efforts. And I always looked, as well, for the person I now knew to be there, but I could never find him.

One morning in early October of that year, I was on Twin Island. As I walked toward the glacial boulder called "Lion Rock" a figure stepped from behind it into my view. He stood and looked at me for what seemed quite a long time before he said, "Good day, I am Joe." I remember thinking, even after those few words, that he had a foreign accent of a sort I had never heard. How mistaken I was! That accent was only foreign to my ears. It was anything else but that to this land of oak trees and blackberries. I didn't know it yet, but I was speaking to a true American, an Algonquin Indian!

The second thing that Joe said was, "I know you very much. You watch all the living things, but you do not harm them. Why?" I tried to explain to him about my interest in natural history and my scouting merit badges, but I think he didn't understand all of it. At some point in our conversation, he decided that scouting was like "being Indian." When that concept had formed in his mind he seemed more at ease with me. Finally, he told me he hoped I would

DIEGO RIVERA

have my merit badges, and he left me to lean on the Lion Rock and wonder. As he walked away I noticed several things about him. His long gray hair and wrinkled face plainly showed great age, but his posture was straight, almost military, with shoulders held stiffly. He was quite tall, perhaps six feet, and lean to the point of boniness. Over his gaunt frame hung a patchwork of clothes made from fur, cloth, and leather.

After that day Joe no longer hid from me, and he would often accompany me on my forays. His knowledge of the woods around us was phenomenal, but he was often confused by my words. If I asked him to show me the heron, he would shrug as if to say "such words are not mine." But if I asked him for the fishing bird with the long neck and pointed beak, he would smile and off we'd go.

In the terms of a modern naturalist, he knew hardly any of the creatures' names. In terms of their lives and hidden places, he knew them all as neighbors. They were his actual, lifelong neighbors, for he had lived here all of his days except for a few years during which he tried unsuccessfully to adapt to the life of New York City and other white man's places.

Joe never actually told me he was an Indian. He seemed to think I should know it automatically, gradually, and that is exactly what happened. I knew. The realization crept up on me over a period of months and finally it was there. I was aware that Joe was an Indian, and somehow, the knowledge did not seem surprising. We had become friends during that winter and when he saw that I had guessed his origins and was still not a threat, he asked if I would hear his story so that it would not die when he went to the Great Spirit. Since all his people were gone now, he knew that when his bones were in the ground no one would be left to speak of him or of his deeds during the storytelling time of future winters. He warned me sternly that Tchi-Manitou, maker of all things, is very strict about the telling of stories. If I ever told the story after he was gone, said Joe, it must only be in the winter, otherwise, the Maker would become angry with me for interrupting the time when His people should fish and plant and put aside food for the long winter. The cold season was the correct time for telling stories.

Gene Schermerhorn
Letters to Phil
1886

It seems hard to believe that Twenty-third Street—which is the first street in the city of which I remember anything, could have changed so much in so short a time. The rural scenes, the open spaces, have vanished; and the small and quiet residences, many of them built entirely of wood, have given place to huge piles of brick and stone, and to iron and plate-glass fronts of the stores which now line the street.

I was six years old when we moved to New York from Williamsburgh in 1848. We went to live in a house in this street just west of Sixth Avenue. It was far out of town then, for people lived about 8th Street, on lower Fifth Avenue, and the cross streets about Washington Square; and even that was considered quite up town, for a great many very nice people lived in Lafayette Place and even in East Broadway and around St. Johns Square.

This will give you an idea of the house; right next door was a small farm or truck-garden extending nearly to Seventh Avenue. Across the way were the stables of the 6th Ave Omnibus line; the stages starting here and going down Sixth Avenue, 8th Street and

Broadway to the Battery. They afterwards started from Forty-sixth Street. I shall have more to tell about these Stage Lines for at this time there were no horse cars. Twenty-third Street and in fact all the streets in the neighborhood were unpaved. Here was my playground and a good one it was. There certainly was plenty of room, plenty of dirt (clean dirt) and plenty of boys; what more could be desired! Of course I was too young at first to enjoy it all as I afterwards did, and your father and Uncle Charlie had most of the fun.

Kite flying, "How Many Miles," marbles and something we called Base Ball were the great games. Think of flying kites now with all the telegraph poles and wires not to speak of the "Cops." Marbles was played in a great ring four or five feet across marked out on the smooth hard dirt; not in the miserable way they do now—a little spot of bare earth about two feet by four and three or four glass marbles, as I saw some boys playing the other day. A handfull or two of marbles were put in the ring; and then you would hear shouts of "knuckle down," "fen dubs," "fen everything," etc. etc. The good shots would have bags half as large as their heads, full of "migs," "China Alleys" and "Real agates." And then a crowd of "Loafers" from some other street would make their appearance, and everyone would grab the marbles and run, or else stand and fight and then there *would* be a time.

But as I say, I was too young to do much more than look on in admiration of my elder brothers. Yet I had some fun too: one of my amusements was to chase the pigs that ran in Sixth Avenue and try (in vain) to catch them with a lassoo made in good shape from old clothes line. Now I suppose a boy would buy a revolver and go west to shoot Indians.

WHEN YOU'RE WRITING

Remember, when you're writing about New York,
Faces are as important as buildings.

Dive deep into the subway, that gallery of portraiture;
Bathe your eyes in that flood of bitter truth.
It is not lovely, it proves no theorems,
But there is no weariness it cannot heal.

Generalizers on human trouble,
Have you courage to face those faces?
You, and you, and you, seen only once,
Good-bye forever, and good luck.

Christopher Morley
from *A Mandarin in New York*
1933

Guido Bruno

'Way Down in Greenwich Village

from *Adventures in American Bookshops, Antique Stores and Auction Rooms*
1922

The fad of false Bohemia in Greenwich Village has passed. The purple and orange brand of tearooms and of so-called gift shops where art lovers and artistic people from the Bronx and Flatbush assembled, have gone out of existence. The designers and manufacturers of astounding atrocities who called themselves "modern artists" have disappeared. True there are a few short-haired women left, who parade the streets in their unusual clothes, but they, too, will soon move to other parts of the city with the return of the soldiers, and will reassume their real calling in life.

Workers and ambitious strivers have taken possession, once more, of the sacred grounds, where memories and hopes are holy possessions, where so many have worked and toiled and spread an evangel, now accepted universally.

New places have sprung up where idlers find themselves isolated, where enthusiasm and sincerity is written on walls and faces. And people are doing things once more in Greenwich Village. Commercialism seems to have disappeared, and men are willing to help men.

Red Smith

The Sporting Life
1964

The saloon at Eighth Avenue and Forty-ninth Street was called the Toy Bulldog. Its proprietor was Mickey Walker, known to sports fans as the Toy Bulldog during the years when he was welterweight champion of the world, when he was middleweight champion of the world, when he tried twice and failed twice to lift the light-heavyweight title from two different champions, when he was belting the brains out of some of the biggest and toughest heavyweights of this century.

Now Mickey Walker was retired and he sat in his saloon drinking whiskey with his friend Francis Albertanti, a small imp who had been a New York sports editor and, later, a publicist for assorted race tracks and fight clubs.

A customer unknown to either tottered from the bar to the table where the pair sat.

"Mickey Walker!" he said. "May I shake your hand?"

Mickey was not displeased.

"Mickey Walker!" the stranger said. "I been watchin' fights all my life. I seen 'em all. Mickey, lemme tell you something. I seen 'em all. Dempsey among the big guys, you among the little guys. The greatest. I seen 'em all and you were the greatest."

Mickey had grown to like this man, but it was Albertanti who spoke. "You say you've seen 'em all," he said. "You ever see Ketchel?"

"Stanley Ketchel!" the man said. "I seen Ketchel a dozen times.

PETER SIS

Maybe two dozen times."

"How do you think Mick, here, would do with Ketchel?" Albertanti asked.

The man recoiled.

"Walker," he said, "you bum, you couldn't whip one side of Ketchel!"

Edith Wharton

The Age of Innocence
1920

"Well—upon my soul!" exclaimed Lawrence Lefferts, turning his opera-glass abruptly away from the stage. Lawrence Lefferts was, on the whole, the foremost authority on "form" in New York. He had probably devoted more time than any one else to the study of this intricate and fascinating question; but study alone could not account for his complete and easy competence. One had only to look at him, from the slant of his bald forehead and the curve of his beautiful fair moustache to the long patent-leather feet at the other end of his lean and elegant person, to feel that the knowledge of "form" must be congenital in any one who knew how to wear such good clothes so carelessly and carry such height with so much lounging grace. As a young admirer had once said of him: "If anybody can tell a fellow just when to wear a black tie with evening clothes and when not to, it's Larry Lefferts." And on the question of pumps versus patent-leather "Oxfords" his authority had never been disputed.

"My God!" he said; and silently handed his glass to old Sillerton Jackson.

Newland Archer, following Lefferts's glance, saw with surprise that his exclamation had been occasioned by the entry of a new figure into old Mrs. Mingott's box. It was that of a slim young woman, a little less tall than May Welland, with brown hair growing in close curls about her temples and held in place by a narrow band of diamonds. The suggestion of this headdress, which gave her what was then called a "Josephine look," was carried out in the

As a token from China.

The English version.

If Germany had presented her.

Irish liberty.

An Anarchistic view.

And how Liberty would have looked as a gift from our own philanthropical millionaires.

HY MAYER

cut of the dark blue velvet gown rather theatrically caught up under her bosom by a girdle with a large old-fashioned clasp. The wearer of this unusual dress, who seemed quite unconscious of the attention it was attracting, stood a moment in the centre of the box, discussing with Mrs. Welland the propriety of taking the latter's place in the front right-hand corner; then she yielded with a slight smile, and seated herself in line with Mrs. Welland's sister-in-law, Mrs. Lovell Mingott, who was installed in the opposite corner.

Mr. Sillerton Jackson had returned the opera-glass to Lawrence Lefferts. The whole of the club turned instinctively, waiting to hear what the old man had to say; for old Mr. Jackson was as great an authority on "family" as Lawrence Lefferts was on "form." He knew all the ramifications of New York's cousinships; and could not only elucidate such complicated questions as that of the connection between the Mingotts (through the Thorleys) with the Dallases of South Carolina, and that of the relationship of the elder branch of Philadelphia Thorleys to the Albany Chiverses (on no account to be confused with the Manson Chiverses of University Place), but could also enumerate the leading characteristics of each family: as, for instance, the fabulous stinginess of the younger lines of Leffertses (the Long Island ones); or the fatal tendency of the Rushworths to make foolish matches; or the insanity recurring in every second generation of the Albany Chiverses, with whom their New York cousins had always refused to intermarry—with the disastrous exception of poor Medora Manson,

who, as everybody knew . . . but then her mother was a Rushworth.

In addition to this forest of family trees, Mr. Sillerton Jackson carried between his narrow hollow temples, and under his soft thatch of silver hair, a register of most of the scandals and mysteries that had smouldered under the unruffled surface of New York society within the last fifty years. So far indeed did his information extend, and so acutely retentive was his memory, that he was supposed to be the only man who could have told you who Julius Beaufort, the banker, really was, and what had become of handsome Bob Spicer, old Mrs. Manson Mingott's father, who had disappeared so mysteriously (with a large sum of trust money) less than a year after his marriage, on the very day that a beautiful Spanish dancer who had been delighting thronged audiences in the old Opera-house on the Battery had taken ship for Cuba. But these mysteries, and many others, were closely locked in Mr. Jackson's breast; for not only did his keen sense of honour forbid his repeating anything privately imparted, but he was fully aware that his reputation for discretion increased his opportunities of finding out what he wanted to know.

The club box, therefore, waited in visible suspense while Mr. Sillerton Jackson handed back Lawrence Lefferts's opera-glass. For a moment he silently scrutinised the attentive group out of his filmy blue eyes overhung by old veined lids; then he gave his moustache a thoughtful twist, and said simply: "I didn't think the Mingotts would have tried it on."

JOE DAVIS

A. J. Liebling

The Telephone Booth Indian

1944

In the Jollity Building, which stands six stories high and covers half of a Broadway block in the high Forties, the term "promoter" means a man who mulcts another man of a dollar, or any fraction or multiple thereof. The verb "to promote" always takes a personal object, and the highest praise you can accord someone in the Jollity Building is to say, "He has promoted some very smart people." The Jollity Building—it actually has a somewhat different name, and the names of its inhabitants are not the ones which will appear below—is representative of perhaps a dozen or so buildings in the upper stories of which the small-scale amusement industry

nests like a tramp pigeon. All of them draw a major part of their income from the rental of their stores at street level, and most of them contain on their lower floors a dance hall or a billiard parlor, or both. The Jollity Building has both. The dance hall, known as Jollity Danceland, occupies the second floor. The poolroom is in the basement. It is difficult in such a building to rent office space to any business house that wants to be taken very seriously, so the upper floors fill up with the petty nomads of Broadway—chiefly orchestra leaders, theatrical agents, bookmakers, and miscellaneous promoters.

Eight coin-box telephone booths in the lobby of the Jollity Building serve as offices for promoters and others who cannot raise the price of desk space on an upper floor. The phones are used mostly for incoming calls. It is a matter of perpetual regret to Morty, the renting agent of the building, that he cannot collect rent from the occupants of the booths. He always refers to them as the Telephone Booth Indians, because in their lives the telephone booth furnishes sustenance as well as shelter, as the buffalo did for the Arapahoe and Sioux. A Telephone Booth Indian on the hunt often tells a prospective investor to call him at a certain hour in the afternoon, giving the victim the number of the phone in one of the booths. The Indian implies, of course, that it is a private line. Then the Indian has to hang in the booth until the fellow calls. To hang, in Indian language, means to loiter. "I used to hang in Forty-sixth Street, front of *Variety*," a small bookmaker may say, referring to a previous business location. Seeing the Indians hanging in the telephone booths is painful to Morty, but there is nothing he can do about it. The regular occupants of the booths recognize one another's rights. It may be understood among them, for instance, that a certain orchestra leader receives calls in a particular booth between three and four in the afternoon and that a competitor has the same booth from four to five. In these circumstances, ethical Indians take telephone messages for each other. There are always fewer vacancies in the telephone booths than in any other part of the Jollity Building.

While awaiting a call, an Indian may occasionally emerge for air, unless the lobby is so crowded that there is a chance he might lose his place to a transient who does not understand the house rules. Usually, however, the Indian hangs in the booth with the door open, leaning against the wall and reading a scratch sheet in order to conserve time. Then, if somebody rings up and agrees to lend him two dollars, he will already have picked a horse on which to lose that amount. When an impatient stranger shows signs of wanting to use a telephone, the man in the booth closes the door, takes the receiver off the hook, and makes motions with his lips, as if talking. To add verisimilitude to a long performance, he occasionally hangs up, takes the receiver down again, drops a nickel in the slot, whirls the dial three or four times, and hangs up again, after which the nickel comes back. Eventually the stranger goes away, and the man in the booth returns to the study of his scratch sheet. . . .

Morty, the renting agent, is a thin, sallow man of forty whose expression has been compared, a little unfairly, to that of a dead robin. He is not, however, a man without feelings; he takes a personal interest in the people who spend much of their lives in the Jollity Building. It is about the same sort of interest that Curator Raymond Ditmars takes in the Bronx Zoo's vampire bats. "I know more heels than any other man in the world," Morty sometimes says, not without pride. "Everywhere I go around Broadway, I get 'Hello, how are you?' Heels that haven't been with me for years, some of them." Morty usually reserves the appellation "heel" for the people who rent the forty-eight cubicles, each furnished with a desk and two chairs, on the third floor of the Jollity Building. These cubicles are formed by partitions of wood and frosted glass which do not quite reach the ceiling. Sufficient air to maintain human life is supposed to circulate over the partitions. The offices rent for $10 and $12.50 a month, payable in advance. "Twelve and a half dollars with air, ten dollars without air," Morty says facetiously. "Very often the heels who rent them take the air without telling me." Sometimes a Telephone Booth Indian acquires enough capital to rent a cubicle. He thus rises in the social scale and becomes a heel. A cubicle has three advantages over a telephone booth. One is that you cannot get a desk into a telephone booth. Another is that you can play pinochle in a cubicle. Another is that a heel gets his name on the directory in the lobby, and the white letters have a bold, legitimate look.

The vertical social structure of the Jollity Building is subject to continual shifts. Not only do Indians become heels, but a heel occasionally accumulates $40 or $50 with which to pay a month's rent on one of the larger offices, all of them unfurnished, on the fourth, fifth, or sixth floor. He then becomes a tenant. Morty always views such progress with suspicion, because it involves sign-

ANDREZJ DUDZINSKI

ing a lease, and once a heel has signed a lease, you cannot put him out without serving a dispossess notice and waiting ten days. A tenant, in Morty's opinion, is just a heel who is planning to get ten days' free rent. "Any time a heel acts prosperous enough to rent an office," Morty says, "you know he's getting ready to take you." A dispossessed tenant often reappears in the Jollity Building as an Indian. It is a life cycle. Morty has people in the building who have been Telephone Booth Indians, heels, and tenants several times each. He likes them best when they are in the heel stage. "You can't collect rent from a guy who hangs in the lobby," he says in explanation, "and with the regular tenant of an unfurnished office, you got too many headaches." He sometimes breaks off a conversation with a friendly heel by saying, "Excuse me, I got to go upstairs and insult a tenant."

Henry Miller
The Ghetto
from *Sexus*
1949

Build your cities proud and high. Lay your sewers. Span your rivers. Work feverishly. Sleep dreamlessly. Sing madly, like the bulbul. Underneath, below the deepest foundations, there lives another race of men. They are dark, somber, passionate. They muscle into the bowels of the earth. They wait with a patience which is terrifying. They are the scavengers, the devourers, the avengers. They emerge when everything topples into dust.

Betty Smith
A Tree Grows in Brooklyn
1943

There was always the music. There were songs and dancing on the Brooklyn streets in those long ago summers and the days should have been joyous. But there was something sad about those summers, something sad about the children, thin in body but with the baby curves still lingering in their faces, singing in sad monotony as they went through the figures of a ring game. It was sad the way they were still babies of four and five years of age but so precocious about taking care of themselves. "The Blue Danube" that the band played was sad as well as bad. The monkey had sad eyes under his bright red cap. The organ grinder's tune was sad under its lilting shrillness.

Even the minstrels who came in the back yards and sang,

If I had my way,
You would never grow old

were sad, too. They were bums and they were hungry and they didn't have talent for song-making. All they had in the world was the nerve to stand in a back yard with cap in hand and sing loudly. The sad thing was in the knowing that all their nerve would get them nowhere in the world and that they were lost as all people in Brooklyn seem lost when the day is nearly over and even though the sun is still bright, it is thin and doesn't give you warmth when it shines on you.

Joe Madden
White Horses en Route to Track
from *Who the Hell Cares?*
1948

This is one of those larceny stories that came to my mind the other night while sitting in my study at home. Arnold Rothstein, the so-called gambler, was, as you all know, one of the most crooked louses in the world. He was born that way, I guess. I coulda wrote a book about this bum, but as he is dead, I'll cut it short and write you one of the stories about him.

As you know, to get to the various race tracks in the metropolitan district, unless you were a "plutocrat," you must ride on the track's Special at the Pennsylvania Railroad. As the boys always wanted action, they coulden wait for the races to start so they could gamble, they devised all sorts of games going to the track. Years ago Long Island had farms all along the railroad tracks and the farmers had horses to do the chores. So the boys would bet on how many brown horses, white, and so on, that they could see from the train window. The more you guess, the bigger the odds. All the big bookmakers would be on the 12:30 train. They, as usual, laid the odds on your guess. Even money if you guessed 10 horses, 13 to 10 on 12, 2 to 1 on 14 and 3 to 1 on 16. 20 horses you would get 5 to 1. They had to be of one color, white being the

horses most popular, as you could easily see 'em.

This Rothstein was beating these bookmakers good on one of these spring meetings. It seemed that all the horses while the 12:30 train went by were swallowed up. The bookies were stuck plenty. Finally they checked up and found out that Rothstein and his agents had bribed all the farmers along the railroad tracks to keep their horses in the barn from 12 to 1:15. He was letting the bookmakers do the guessing and the picking. So the boys had to get even. They did one day. They all bet Rothstein a fortune. They sed it ran into close to $50,000.

That day it seemed that all the white horses in the world were in Long Island on the farms alongside the railroad tracks. To make sure that there woulden be any mistakes the stooges for the bookmakers dressed as farmers, had the horses right in front so there woulden be any beefs. They counted 32 white horses that day. And, folks, that was the end of betting on the horses on the trains. One bookmaker, after he collected, cracked to Rothstein, "We sure were lucky, Arnold; guess the white horses had a convention on Long Island today."

Russell Baker
The Night the Lights Went Out
1965

Russell Baker, writing for the editorial page of *The Times*, gazed into the future and came up with this vision:

"The end came on Sept. 17, 1973. It had been forecast by an M.I.T. undergraduate who had been running the law of probability through his computer.

"The frequency of malfunction in New York, his computer noted, had increased at such a rate that an ultimate day of total breakdown was a statistical certainty by the early 1970's. Naturally, no one took the forecast as anything more than an undergraduate hoax.

"The chain of events on that last day began at Shea Stadium at 4:43 P.M. when the Mets finished a scoreless ninth inning against the Mexico City Braves, thus becoming the first team in history to lose 155 games in a single baseball season.

"Two minutes later, Irma Arnstadt, a Bronx housewife, turned on the kitchen faucet and noticed that there was no water. Going to the telephone, she dialed her plumber, not knowing that at that very moment, in defiance of the law of probability, 6,732,548 other persons in New York were simultaneously dialing telephone numbers.

"Mrs. Arnstadt's call was the one that broke the system's back. Somewhere in a sealed, windowless building a transistor gasped and failed. Under the incredible overload, other transistors all over the city groaned and gave up. And so, with the telephones out, it was hours before the authorities could learn that there was not a drop of water left anywhere in the pipes of the five boroughs.

"The press might have detected it almost immediately, but, as chance would have it, the biennial newspaper strike began that day at 5 P.M. and not a single newspaperman was on duty.

"At 5:03 P.M. outside the Waldorf-Astoria Hotel, a taxi driver was shot by a man who had been trying unsuccessfully for fifty-five minutes to get a cab. It was later established that the man had been trying futilely to find an empty cab during the rush hour in Man-

ANTON VAN DALEN

hattan for sixteen years. 'I just snapped,' he said later. 'That was a day when everything seemed to just snap.'

"News of the shooting spread rapidly through the city's cab fleet. Panic seized the drivers who feared a general uprising by the rush-hour hordes signaling in vain for taxicabs. As a result the drivers abandoned their hacks in the streets.

"By 5:30 P.M. the resulting traffic jam extended from Trenton to New Haven. Two minutes later, a radio sports reporter announced that the Yankees had dropped their fourth in a row to the Milwaukee Athletics and were, thus, once again mathematically eliminated from any possibility of finishing in the first division.

"This news was interrupted by a bulletin reporting that more than fifty knifings had occurred simultaneously on fifty different subway trains scattered throughout the city and that the subway trainmen had walked out on a wildcat strike to press demands for more police protection.

"At City Hall, there was no hint that anything untoward was happening until 5:12 P.M. when it began to snow. The Mayor watched the snow for perhaps twenty minutes and then summoned his press adviser. 'What is that?' he asked, pointing out the window. 'Snow, your Honor,' said the press adviser, who was one of the brighter products of the Democratic machine that had been returned to power after John Lindsay had gone on to more manageable tasks than governing New York.

"The Mayor was aggrieved. 'In the old days, when the machine

was running this city right,' said the Mayor, 'it never snowed in September.' 'True,' said the press adviser, 'but the machine is like everything else in New York these days. It doesn't work.'

"All over the city, with no water left in the pipes, no subways running, no telephone service, no newspapers, the snow pouring down and both the Mets and the Yankees dead, people felt in a gay festive mood. And so, as people will under hardship, millions decided to spend a night on the town.

"In the theater district alone, 500,000 people appeared at box offices demanding theater tickets, which then retailed at $79.90 per seat. With vast lines at every box office, the manager of a theater in 43rd Street announced at 8:22 P.M. that there were no tickets available for anybody without enough influence to rate a good table at Twenty-One.

"New Yorkers, being New Yorkers, might not have broken even then, except for a Brooklyn man named Omar. At that moment in Brooklyn, Omar plugged in his electric carving knife and the entire Atlantic seaboard from Labrador to Chattanooga was plugged into blackness.

"By next morning, of course—we all know the story—volunteers began bringing out the first New York survivors, and six days later the President viewed the area in a flying inspection tour and ordered his historic re-evaluation of American civilization.

"Which, as everybody knows, is why nobody lives in cities any more."

In Transit

Joseph Mitchell
My Ears Are Bent
1938

Early in February, 1934, more than 12,000 taxicab drivers went on strike. I was sent out to ride around town in cabs driven by scabs. I wasn't told to find out why the scabs were scabbing, or anything as pertinent as that; I was sent out to get an amusing story. In such an occurrence as a citywide taxicab strike the function of the feature writer is to pimp for the status quo. The feature editor, in fact, told me to ask the drivers to talk about their adventures with drunks, and to find out what class of citizens are the poorest tippers; such things as that. I got into the first cab at a street corner on lower Broadway. I gave an address in Brooklyn, and the driver jerked the flag down.

"It's right near Borough Hall," I said. "What do you know about the strike?"

"I haven't had time to read the papers," said the driver, who was, according to his license card, Henry Kopf. "I guess it's going all right. I own my own cab, and I try not to have nothing to do with them unions. If you're on the wrong side they tear your cab up, and

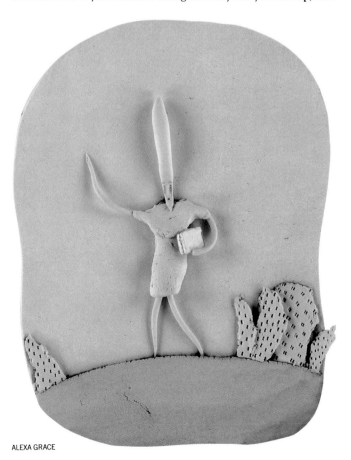

ALEXA GRACE

if you're on the right side you got to tear somebody else's cab up. I don't want to tear no cabs up."

"Have you had any trouble during the strike?"

"Well, no. One night some of them strikers tried to wreck my cab, but I had four drunk passengers and they got out and beat the hell out of the strikers. I never saw such fighting and yelling."

The cab sped over Brooklyn Bridge. Mr. Kopf drove slowly, and talked about his future.

"I mean to get out of this racket very soon," he said. "I mean you get tired of riding around town with a lot of drunks and yelling women. My wife's brother owns a chicken farm three miles out in the country from Kingston, and I'm saving up to go in with him."

A few minutes later I got into another cab.

"No, I don't know how the strike is going," said the driver, John Carlsen, of 960 Third Ave. "It's just another run-around."

"Have you ever had any adventures driving a cab?" he was asked.

"Plenty," he said. "One night this winter a guy jumped in my cab at Sheridan Sq. and said he wanted me to drive him to the East River and throw him in. I asked him did he have any money. He said he had plenty of money, but he didn't have anything to live for. He threw his pocketbook through my window, and I stopped and counted and he had $61. So I said, 'What the hell do you mean you got nothing to live for? There's $61 in here.'

"But he said I didn't understand. He said he wanted to commit suicide, but he was afraid he wouldn't jump in when he got to the water and he wanted somebody to throw him in. I figured I would get a fare out of him. So I drove up to the foot of E. 42nd St., which is a good place to jump into the East River, and I yelled to him that he could jump out there. He didn't answer, and I saw he was fast asleep.

"So I drove around and found a cop, and I said, 'I got a guy in here that asked me to throw him into the East River.' The cop thought I was nuts. Anyhow, we looked through the guy's pockets, and got his address. So I drove him home. He lived over on Prospect Park West, in Brooklyn. Well, I got him out and me and the doorman took him upstairs.

"I told his wife about the whole thing, and so she paid me off and gave me a dime tip. She said, 'That's all I'm going to tip you, just a dime. If you had thrown him in I would have given you a $5 tip.'"

Then I got into a taxicab equipped with a radio. It was driven by Ignatz A. Weinstein, who said he lived in a furnished room at 402 8th Ave., and that he used to be an advertising solicitor, and that he barely made a living.

Mr. Weinstein was asked what class of citizens give the lowest tips.

"It has been my experience," he said, speaking slowly and deliberately, "that the worst tippers are society women and preachers."

"What kind of music do you like to hear over your radio?" I asked.

"The kind of music I like to hear," said Mr. Weinstein, reaching over and slapping his clicking meter, "is the music made by this here thing."

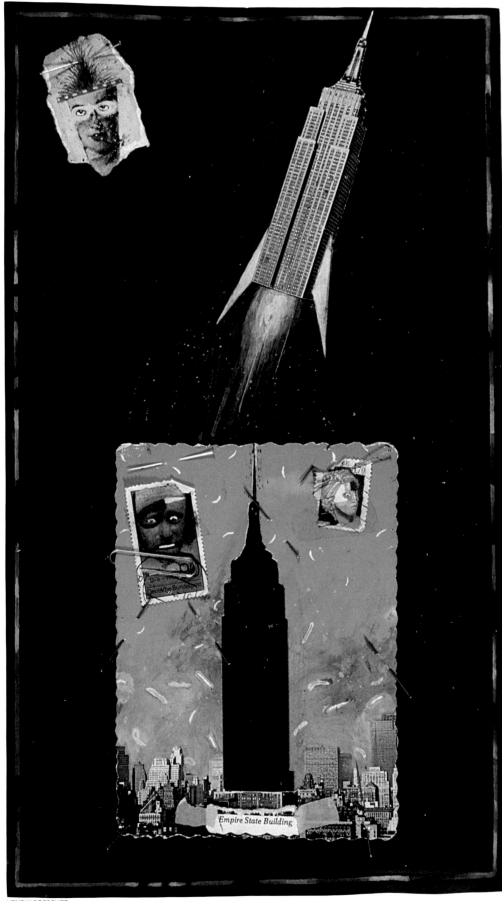

HENRIK DRESCHER

STOW WENGENROTH

William Dean Howells

A Hazard of New Fortunes

1890

At Third Avenue they took the elevated, for which she confessed an infatuation. She declared it the most ideal way of getting about in the world, and was not ashamed when he reminded her of how she used to say that nothing under the sun could induce her to travel on it. She now said that the night transit was even more interesting than the day, and that the fleeting intimacy you formed with people in second- and third-floor interiors, while all the usual street life went on underneath, had a domestic intensity mixed with a perfect repose that was the last effect of good society with all its security and exclusiveness. He said it was better than the theater, of which it reminded him, to see those people through their windows: a family party of workfolk at a late tea, some of the men in their shirt-sleeves; a woman sewing by a lamp; a mother laying her child in its cradle; a man with his head fallen on his hands upon a table; a girl and her lover leaning over the windowsill together. What suggestion! What drama! What infinite interest!

At the Forty-second Street station they stopped a minute on the bridge that crosses the track to the branch road for the Central Depot, and looked up and down the long stretch of the elevated to north and south. The track that found and lost itself a thousand times in the flare and tremor of the innumerable lights; the moony sheen of the electrics mixing with the reddish points and blots of gas far and near; the architectural shapes of houses and churches and towers, rescued by the obscurity from all that was ignoble in them; and the coming and going of the trains marking the stations with vivider or fainter plumes of flame-shot steam—formed an incomparable perspective. They often talked afterward of the superb spectacle, which in a city full of painters nightly works its unrecorded miracles; and they were just to the Arachne roof spun in iron over the cross street on which they ran to the depot; but for the present they were mostly inarticulate before it. They had another moment of rich silence when they paused in the gallery that leads from the elevated station to the waiting rooms in the Central Depot and looked down upon the great night trains lying on the tracks dim under the rain of gaslights that starred without dispersing the vast darkness of the place. What forces, what fates, slept in these bulks which would soon be hurling themselves north and east and west through the night! Now they waited there like fabled monsters of Arab story ready for the magician's touch, tractable, reckless, will-less—organized lifelessness full of a strange semblance of life.

Cecil Beaton

Cecil Beaton's New York

1938

New York appears to be a great city in a great hurry. The average street pace must surely be forty miles an hour. The traffic lights switch straight from red to green and green to red, without any nonsense about orange, symbolising the harshness of contrast that dispenses with the intermediary things that Europeans respect. It is usually unwise to cross the road except in accordance with the green light, and even New York dogs are said to understand this symbol. Americans always know their cue, as they know when to throw in the gear just before the light goes green.

Mark Twain

The Sex in New York

from *Mark Twain's Travels with Mr. Brown*
1867

Editors Alta: They do not treat women with as much deference in New York as we of the provinces think they ought. This is painfully apparent in the street-cars. Authority winks at the overloading of the cars—authority being paid for so winking, in political influence, possibly, for I cannot bring myself to think that any other species of bribery would be entertained for a moment—authority, I say, winks at this outrage, and permits one car to do the work of at least two, instead of compelling the companies to double the number of their cars, and permits them, also, to cruelly over-work their horses, too, of course, in the face of the Society for the Prevention of Cruelty to Animals. The result of this over-crowding is to set the people back a long stride toward semi-civilization. What I mean by that dreadful assertion is, that the over-crowding of the cars has impelled men to adopt the rule of hanging on to a seat when they get it, though twenty beautiful women came in and stood in their midst. That is going back toward original barbarism, I take it. A car's proper cargo should be twenty-two inside and three upon each platform—twenty-eight—and no crowding. I have seen fifty-six persons on a car, here, but a large portion of them were hanging on by the teeth. Some of the men inside had to go four or five miles, and naturally enough did not like to give up their seats and stand in a packed mass of humanity all that distance. So, when a lady got in, no man offered her a seat—no man dreamt of doing such a thing. No citizen, I mean. Occasionally I have seen a man, under such circumstances, get up and give his place to a lady, but the act betrayed, like spoken words, that he was from the provinces. . . .

The other day an ill-bred boy in a street-car refused to give up his seat to a lady. The conductor very properly snatched him out and seated the lady. Consequence: Justice Dowling fined that *conductor* a month's wages—sixty dollars—and read him a lecture worth sixty dollars more.

JOHN HELD, JR.

GRAND CENTRAL STATION

The clock hath tolled the hour of ten o'clock;
At five past ten the train we take departs,
When suddenly my wife, as is her wont,
Whenever week-end visiting we go
Exclaims in tragic, anguished tones "Oh Hell!
I haven't bought a solitary thing
For Marjorie, for Betty or for Bill."
Then, like a deer affrighted by the hounds,
Like arrows speeding swiftly from the bow,
With frantic haste we rush and tear about,
And purchase make, nor dare to wait for change,
Until, at last, we, breathless, board the train.
We hear the gateman's strident "All aboard!"
As limp and worn we sink into our seats.
But from our hearts there comes a grateful song,
"Thank God, thank God for Liggetts!" we exclaim.

Newman Levy and John Held, Jr.
from *From Saturday to Monday*
1930

BASCOVE

Herman Melville

First Night of Their Arrival in the City

from *Pierre*
1852

The stage was belated.

The country road they travelled entered the city by a remarkably wide and winding street, a great thoroughfare for its less opulent inhabitants. There was no moon and few stars. It was that preluding hour of the night when the shops are just closing, and the aspect of almost every wayfarer, as he passes through the unequal light reflected from the windows, speaks of one hurrying not abroad, but homeward. Though the thoroughfare was winding, yet no sweep that it made greatly obstructed its long and imposing vista; so that when the coach gained the top of the long and very gradual slope running toward the obscure heart of the town, and the twinkling perspective of two long and parallel rows of lamps was revealed—lamps which seemed not so much intended to dispel the general gloom, as to show some dim path leading through it, into some gloom still deeper beyond;—when the coach gained this critical point, the whole vast triangular town, for a moment, seemed dimly and despondently to capitulate to the eye.

And now, ere descending the gradually sloping declivity and just on its summit as it were, the inmates of the coach, by numerous hard, painful joltings, and ponderous dragging trundlings, are suddenly made sensible of some great change in the character of the road. The coach seems rolling over cannon-balls of all calibers. Grasping Pierre's arm, Isabel eagerly and forebodingly demands what is the cause of this most strange and unpleasant transition.

'The pavements, Isabel; this is the town.'

Isabel was silent.

But, the first time for many weeks, Delly voluntarily spoke:

'It feels not so soft as the green sward, Master Pierre.'

'No, Miss Ulver,' said Pierre, very bitterly, 'the buried hearts of some dead citizens have perhaps come to the surface.'

'Sir?' said Delly.

'And are they so hard-hearted here?' asked Isabel.

'Ask yonder pavements, Isabel. Milk dropped from the milkman's can in December, freezes not more quickly on those stones, than does snow-white innocence, if in poverty it chance to fall in these streets.'

'Then God help my hard fate, Master Pierre,' sobbed Delly. 'Why didst thou drag hither a poor outcast like me?'

'Forgive me, Miss Ulver,' exclaimed Pierre, with sudden warmth, and yet most marked respect; 'forgive me; never yet have I entered the city by night, but, somehow, it made me feel both bitter and sad. Come, be cheerful, we shall soon be comfortably housed, and have our comfort all to ourselves; the old clerk I spoke to you about, is now doubtless ruefully eyeing his hat on the peg. Come, cheer up, Isabel;—'tis a long ride, but here we are, at last. Come! 'Tis not very far now to our welcome.'

'I hear a strange shuffling and clattering,' said Delly, with a shudder.

'It does not seem so light as just now,' said Isabel.

'Yes,' returned Pierre, 'it is the shop-shutters being put on; it is the locking, and bolting, and barring of windows and doors; the

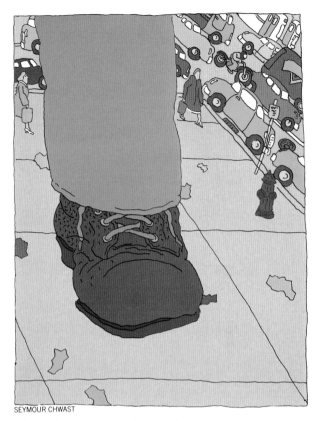

SEYMOUR CHWAST

town's-people are going to their rest.'

'Please God they may find it!' sighed Delly.

'They lock and bar out, then, when they rest, do they, Pierre?' said Isabel.

'Yes, and you were thinking that does not bode well for the welcome I spoke of.'

'Thou read'st all my soul; yes, I was thinking of that. But whither lead these long, narrow, dismal side-glooms we pass every now and then? What are they? They seem terribly still. I see scarce anybody in them;—there's another, now. See how haggardly look its criss-cross, far-separate lamps.—What are these side-glooms, dear Pierre; whither lead they?'

'They are the thin tributaries, sweet Isabel, to the great Orinoco thoroughfare we are in; and like true tributaries, they come from the far-hidden places; from under dark beetling secrecies of mortar and stone through the long marsh-grasses of villainy, and by many a transplanted bough-beam, where the wretched have hung.'

'I know nothing of these things, Pierre. But I like not the town. Think'st thou, Pierre, the time will ever come when all the earth shall be paved?'

'Thank God, that never can be!'

'These silent side-glooms are horrible;—look! Methinks, not for the world would I turn into one.'

That moment the nigh fore-wheel sharply grated under the body of the coach.

'Courage!' cried Pierre, 'we are in it!—Not so very solitary either; here comes a traveller.'

'Hark, what is that?' said Delly, 'that keen iron-ringing sound? It passed us just now.'

'The keen traveller,' said Pierre, 'he has steel plates to his boot-heels;—some tender-souled elder son, I suppose.'

'Pierre,' said Isabel, 'this silence is unnatural, is fearful. The forests are never so still.'

Christopher Morley
Swiss Family Manhattan
1932

It was early, and I rambled without purpose, interesting myself by going contrary to the larger currents of population, as in that way I could better watch the faces. Unusually dense files of people were moving through the crossways ravines, and presently I noted that they were emerging in thousands from a central subterranean cavern. It was hard to tell from their disciplined countenances whether they were escaping from or hurrying toward. Some obscure but methodical convulsion was at work, for they issued not in continuous flow but in successive squads. Suddenly they would pour up thick from the various gangways, pressing intently, even gladly, like those quit of a sombre experience; then, as though some vast pressure were momentarily removed, there came only a few stragglers, the obese, the halt, or the derelict. Then again the stairs were filled with urgent masses who crowded forth and without pause or sideward look went steadily pattering to

their employment. They lived by rule; theirs, I learned later, was the highest meed of praise, regular fellows. The very iron of the treads was worn and brightened by their millions of regular feet.

I could not be satisfied as to the meaning of this phenomenon until I made my way down and found a large underground railway. With the even rhythm of great pistons in a pumping system trains of cars slid to and fro. From distant conduits they sucked in their human packing, shot the swaying masses to central arteries, discharged them through clattering turnstiles which enumerated the herd and propelled any who sought to delay with a genial postern whack.

Nothing could be more gloomy, grim, or sordid than these dark railroads, constructed evidently for the punishment of those not wise or wealthy enough to live within easy reach of their labor, but valuable also for the bewilderment of strangers. The cars were like prison vans, but some humane attempt had been made to distract the victims, for even here they were not entirely deprived of what they enjoy and understand: the solicitations of advertising, small sweetmeats, and newspapers. It was seemingly always their hope that even during the brief duration of their underground passage something exciting might have happened, for at every station there were fresh newspapers, and magazines specializing in the more obvious consolations of love and hygiene. They were innocently unaware that love is an elusive essence that rarely gets into

ANDREZJ CZECOT

print; and hardly ever (by some very obscure law) on printed pages measuring larger than 6 inches by 9. The very hardy might also keep up their morale by seeing themselves in small mirrors attached to candy machines. Not having made a careful toilet for two days, I desired to consult one of these mirrors and consider the set of my beard, but I did not know whether it might be held dishonorable to use the glass without buying the candy. I attempted to inquire of the official at the money-window, but while I was trying to formulate the question he waved me away for delaying his clients.

At the cost of only a small coin I studied this extraordinary penal system for a long while. The trains exercised enormous fascination upon their passengers, who poured in like devotees impassioned with ecstasy; through perilous narrow apertures of almost-closed doors they thrust and wiggled; all, even children and old beldames, gained that sanctuary with an air of triumph, burrowed into the close-wedged throng, and relapsed into their sincerest piety, the adoration of haste. Nowhere, in spite of their discomforts, did I observe ill temper or indignation. It was evident that the natives had been so well trained that it never even occurred to them that all this was fantastic and appalling. I concluded that given enough lithographs of underwear and canned victual they will endure anything.

Helen Keller
Midstream
1929

Tremulously I stand in the subways, absorbed into the terrible reverberations of exploding energy. Fearful, I touch the forest of steel girders loud with the thunder of oncoming trains that shoot past me like projectiles. Inert I stand, riveted in my place. My limbs, paralyzed, refuse to obey the will insistent on haste to board the train while the lightning steed is leashed and its reeling speed checked for a moment. Before my mind flashes in clairvoyant vision what all this speed portends—the lightning crashing into life, the accidents, railroad wrecks, steam bursting free like geysers from bands of steel, thousands of racing motors and children caught at play, flying heroes diving into the sea, dying for speed—all this because of strange, unsatisfied ambitions. Another train bursts into the station like a volcano, the people crowd me on, on into the chasm—into the dark depths of awful forces and fates. In a few minutes, still trembling, I am spilled into the streets.

ANDREZJ CZECOT

ROBERT NEUBECKER

The Fulton Ferry

from *New York Mirror*, January 2, 1836

It is not pleasant, nor is it sometimes safe, to cross a river in a ferryboat crowded with carriages, carts, horses, etc., and we have often wondered why separate and distinct boats were not provided for the accommodation of all parties, more particularly at a ferry so much frequented as that at the foot of Fulton Street. The decks of these boats are not unfrequently jammed with a heterogeneous mass of live and dead stock; hucksters and their miscellanies; milkmen with their pans; hay-carts, wagons, drays, men, women, children, pigs, sheep, ducks, pigeons, geese, eggs, hens, clean and unclean things, all promiscuously huddled together, and affording a miniature view of the interior of the ark of old. This might be obviated by appropriating the present boats exclusively to the accommodation of the market people, and such others as may have produce or merchandise to transport in vehicles or otherwise; and by adding a couple of neat and comfortable boats, with warm and commodious deck apartments, for the exclusive conveyance of unencumbered pedestrians. This ought to be done, and at this season of the year iceboats should be procured, and, in short, every facility afforded the publick by the holders of a monopoly so lucrative as the Fulton-street ferry-company.

Theodore Dreiser
The Color of a Great City

1923

Have you ever arisen at dawn or earlier in New York and watched the outpouring in the meaner side-streets or avenues? It is a wondrous thing. It seems to have so little to do with the later, showier, brisker life of the day, and yet it has so very much. It is in the main so drab or shabby-smart at best, poor copies of what you see done more efficiently later in the day. Typewriter girls in almost stage or society costumes entering shabby offices; boys and men made up to look like actors and millionaires turning into the humblest institutions, where they are clerks or managers. These might be called the machinery of the city, after the elevators and street cars and wagons are excluded, the implements by which things are made to go. . . .

Already at six and six-thirty in the morning they have begun to trickle small streams of human beings Manhattan or cityward, and by seven and seven-fifteen these streams have become sizable affairs. By seven-thirty and eight they have changed into heavy, turbulent rivers, and by eight-fifteen and eight-thirty and nine they are raging torrents, no less. They overflow all the streets and avenues and every available means of conveyance. They are pouring into all available doorways, shops, factories, office-buildings —those huge affairs towering so significantly above them. Here they stay all day long, causing those great hives and their adjacent streets to flush with a softness of color not indigenous to them, and then at night, between five and six, they are going again, pouring forth over the bridges and through the subways and across the ferries and out on the trains, until the last drop of them appears to have been exuded, and they are pocketed in some outlying side-street or village or metropolitan hall-room—and the great, turbulent night of the city is on once more.

BROADWAY

What hurrying human tides, or day or night!
What passions, winnings, losses, ardors, swim thy waters!
What whirls of evil, bliss and sorrow, stem thee!
What curious questioning glances—glints of love!
Leer, envy, scorn, contempt, hope, aspiration!
Thou portal—thou arena—thou of the myriad long-drawn
    lines and groups!
(Could but thy flagstones, curbs, façades, tell their inimitable
    tales;
Thy windows rich, and huge hotels—thy side-walks wide;)
Thou of the endless sliding, mincing, shuffling feet!
Thou, like the parti-colored world itself—like infinite,
    teeming, mocking life!
Thou visor'd, vast, and unspeakable show and lesson!

                  Walt Whitman
                  from *Leaves of Grass*
                  1888

Joel H. Ross, M.D.
What I Saw in New-York
1851

RECKLESS DRIVING

But we not only see much in this street to amuse us, but some things to annoy and provoke us. While standing on the walk in the upper part of the street, where pedestrians and others are much less numerous than in the lower part, I saw two dandies in a light wagon coming up, driving a span of horses most furiously, which made me fear that somebody would get hurt by their dangerous and unjustifiable speed. And this made me watch them the closer.

A lad, about half way to manhood, was standing in the middle of the street, without any apparent inclination to pass to either side. He appeared to see the vehicle approaching, yet made no more effort to get out of the way than if he had been a statue. This, I confess, made me a little nervous. The driver evidently saw him, for the boy then had the street all to himself. And yet he never made the least attempt to check his horses or change their course, and hence contact was unavoidable.

The horses knocked him down, and gave him so much momentum, that horses, wagon, boy and all went on together I should

think at least a rod, and I could hardly tell which rolled the better or the faster, the boy or the wheels. The horses passed over him as well as they could, and the wagon too; the boy jumped up and started off, and glad to get off so; the rascal of a driver never checked his horses, nor turned his head to see whether the boy was dead or alive; and I could have seen the big key of "Sing Sing" turned upon him with an excellent relish. . . .

SCENE IN AN OMNIBUS

A world in miniature is a stage load of passengers, and more than once have I been greatly amused in such a company; and to make the variety all the greater, I have sometimes been a little *annoyed*.

Once on a day of bustling commotion, when stacks of mud dotted the streets and bespattered the sidewalks, I took my seat in one of these velveted vehicles with a strong inclination to make the most of a ride through Broadway, and get the worth of my money, which, perhaps, I ought to tell the reader, who is not in the habit of riding in such modern carts, was six and quarter cents, more or less.

Well, after the driver had stopped and started, and opened and shut his clattering cage fifteen or sixteen times, with a little squeezing, scolding and scowling, we had a load of men, women and children, in silks and rags—bankers and brokers, tinkers and tailors, laborers and lawyers, &c.

I said that squeezing was a part of the process of stage packing, and although a little unpleasant, it seems to be quite indispensable, and for at least three reasons. In the first place, it is hard for the driver to believe that twelve seats are ever *all* occupied. I have seen him with his characteristic philanthropy, throw open his door to the weary traveller, when almost every seat and lap within was well nigh twice occupied, though the party of which I am now speaking, did not happen to be quite so numerous.

Then, the fair sex—bless their hearts, they don't intend any harm by it—sometimes forget that they expect to pay for only a single seat. This subjects others to a little extra compression, though they be not fond of "tight lacing."

Again, the *un*fair sex, after being comfortably seated, sometimes seem never to suspect that the omnibus was ever made for anybody else. But any way to get a ride.

Edward Sorel

The Rise and Fall of the Taxi

1984

We have come to expect schools, subways and public libraries to deteriorate. After all, they are used by the poor, and the poor can't afford lobbyists. But taxis are used by the well-to-do, who as a rule know how to protect their privileges and comforts. So it is surprising to see our City Fathers conferring taxi medallions on fiendishly uncomfortable vehicles and issuing hack licenses to rude and slovenly drivers. Perhaps this governmental unconcern with the haves as well as the have-nots means that democracy is better than ever. God knows, taxis aren't.

3.

2.

1.

1. ORIGIN OF SPECIES... The first motorized taxis, at the turn of the century, retained much of the look and feel of horse-drawn hansoms, including the comfort of having the driver outside the cab. A good start.

2. DISARMAMENT... By the twenties, having just finished fighting "to make the world safe for democracy," Americans decided to let the driver share the cab space with the passenger, raising questions as to whether the war was worth fighting.

3. THE ENLIGHTENMENT... Sun roofs were standard in Europe by the time De Soto brought out its version in 1936. The lore is that New Yorkers called them "sunshine cabs" because the largest fleet of them (2,300) was the Sunshine Radio Systems Association.

4.

4. THE GOLDEN AGE... In the late thirties, with millions still unemployed, the cabby valued his job and needed your tips. As a result, he helped you with your packages, opened doors, and said quaint things like "Thank you."

5. ON THE HOME FRONT... During World War II the few cabs that were still around rattled with age and neglect, and the drivers were Army rejects. The terrible part of it was that we got used to it.

6. AT THIS POINT IN TIME... By the seventies the taxis had come round full circle. The partition has returned, this time in bulletproof plastic and no longer for the benefit of the passenger. The driver, who is now unionized, has all the leg room up front and employs his off-duty sign as a means to reject any passengers who are not going in his direction. *Sic transit gloria* transit.

5.

6.

Isaac S. Lyon
Recollections of an Old Cartman
1872

A New York cartman, above all others, should be an honest, intelligent and upright man—for he must necessarily be entrusted with untold wealth in one shape and another. I recollect having on my cart one afternoon property valued at half a million of dollars, be the same more or less. It consisted of a collection of about thirty dingy-looking old oil paintings—said to be the grandest productions of some of the so-called old masters. I never once doubted the genuineness of their *antiquity*; but, although I had plenty of money in my pocket at the time, I wish to have it distinctly understood that I did not purchase them at that price. And right here permit me to remark—not under oath, however—that I acquired a very high character for honesty and square dealing during the twenty years that I followed carting; indeed so *high* that I have not yet, with all my subsequent practice, become a very expert thief, which fact almost debars me from obtaining my rightful dues in this thieving and grab-game age.

The business of a catch cartman calls him in every direction, all over the city, into the damp and loathsome vaults of the dead, and all through the stately marble palaces of the living, into the attics of six-story hotels, and down to the fish-smelling wharfs, whence the "people" go down to the sea in ships. His daily beat comprises not only the city proper but all the surrounding country for twenty miles or more round about. Everybody trusts the cartman—oftentimes with secrets that they would not have divulged for the world—and it is very seldom that their trust is betrayed. His cartman's frock, and his honest, open countenance is a sufficient passport for him to go unchallenged wherever he pleases, and there is no one to say to him, "thus far mayest thou go and no further." And no matter where he goes, whether it be into the vaults of a bank or a lady's dressing-room, everybody supposes that *it's all right* and that he has been sent there by somebody on business, and no one questions him for being there. Oftentimes ladies of the *very highest* standing—sometimes standing as *high* as five feet six in their gaiters—confide secrets to their cartman such as they would not *dare* to intrust to their husbands, and much less to their servant girls. A cartman who has established a good character for honesty and intelligence is looked upon by most business men as a person of more than ordinary importance, and treated accordingly.

During the last two weeks in April of each year the cartmen begin to put on a few extra airs, and look and act with more importance than at any other time during the year. Everybody then calls him *Mr.* Cartman, and when the first day of May arrives then "stand from under!" He then becomes very domineering, and everybody feels that it is their interest, if not their duty, to bow and cringe to him, for on that day of all the year it is generally admitted that a cartman may charge any price that he pleases. Through a long continued practice this has become a fixed custom, which no one presumes to call in question, although there is no law in existence that justifies this assumption. All the goods and personal property, as well as a large portion of the real, contained within the city limits have passed through the hands of the New York cartmen at one time or another, and I fully believe that, were the

truth of the case known, more wealth passes through the hands of the city cartmen every year than is handled by the whole board of Wall street brokers.

It is generally expected that a cartman should know everybody and everything—here, there and everywhere—past, present and to come. He must know the exact locations of all public and business places—theatres and hotels, factories and workshops, shipping points and railroad depots—what time this ship sails, and what time that train starts, and whether there are any *runaway couples* on board of either. He must know in what streets all the churches and justices' courts are located; to what denomination each church belongs, and who preaches in them; the name of the presiding justice in each court, and how large a fee it will require to bribe each of them. He must know where to find all the colleges and schoolhouses, the names of the professors in this college, and of the teachers in that schoolhouse; who lives here, and who lives there; when this man is going to move, and where that man has moved to. He is likewise expected to know all the doctors, both quack and regular, and which can make the largest blue pills, and which can saw off your leg without your knowing it. Also, all the choice city scandal, and who has been fortunate enough to see the elephant; who is going to elope with this man's wife, and who is going to run away with that man's daughter. In fact, it is generally expected by all those who know nothing themselves that the New York cartman should be an encyclopaedia and an intelligence office combined; and if he don't happen to know all this and a great deal more, he is set down as a know-nothing, and asked why he don't go to school and learn his A, B, C's? But almost any sharp, wide-awake cartman, who has taken out the first renewal of his license, would be able to answer all these questions correctly, and a great many more which it would not be prudent for some gentlemen, who value their domestic peace, to ask.

* * *

And now, reader, what think you of New York city as it *was* and *is*? There is not another place like it in all the world; and "with all its faults I love it still;" for it presents to the world one of the most striking exemplifications of what a *free* and enterprising people can do when they set themselves about it. New York is what might be most emphatically termed a *fast* city. Yes! the very *fastest* in all creation. Its men are *fast*, its women are *fast*, and so are its horses. Its merchants are *fast*, its brokers are *fast*, and so are its swindlers. Its steamships are *fast*, its railroads are *fast*, and so are its politicians. Its churches are *fast*, its theatres are *fast*, and so are its saints

and sinners. Everything goes with a *rush*—everybody is always in a *hurry*—and any man who is of the city-born, can always recognize a fellow New Yorker in any part of the world, by the *fastness* of his movements. I have seen a *fast* man, with a *fast* horse and sleigh, jump over a cartman's sled, without doing any damage to either—*and nobody to blame*. I have known men to leave their offices in the afternoon, worth hundreds of thousands of dollars, and wake up the next morning not worth a cent—and nobody made any richer by the loss. New York is a *fast* place in every sense of the word. It's a *fast* place to make money in, and a *fast* place to spend it—a *fast* place to live in, and a *fast* place to die in. Justice and Religion are the only two dignitaries that drive a *slow* coach—and under the present organization of society *they* could not drive fast if they wished to.

Sean O'Casey

Rose and Crown

1952

On that same calm evening, when the moon rode high, George Jean Nathan guided him towards the one hansom cab left living in the world. There it stood, wisting not of the new world's ways, cab, horse, and driver, embedded in time that had stood still for them; close to the kerb of a sidewalk in a measureless street running past a threatening towering hotel, racing on ahead of life, and pushing its way out of the past of a year ago. There they waited, an *il penseroso* of forgotten days; jarred in a jellied time within the surrounding epic of living steel, concrete, and stone. A dreaming ghost of Fergus Hume's *Mystery of a Hansom Cab*. The serious critic and the serious dramatist, the man from Indiana and the man from Dublin, climbed into the cab for a jaunt through a park in the moonlight. Away they went through Central Park to the tune of clop-cloppety-clop of the hansom's horse, valiantly keeping his tail up; the beetling buildings surrounding them looking like stony titans watching two of their titan children taking an evening airing in a huge old-fashioned pram with its big hood up like the horsey's tail; the buildings, ebony where the moonlight shone not, quietly candescent with a primrose silver shade where the moonlight fell; cloppety-clop now through a patch of gloom, then through a glade marred delightfully by a crop of rugged rock spurting up through the delicate grass, glazed over with soft moonlight and sad, shining like a light from a lantern carried by a god looking for a lost and lovely goddess.

The horse, the cab, and the driver sent ghosts of the past sidling up to Sean; shadows of the time when men's eyes sought the jutting bustle, and whose ears listened for the frou-frou of the trailing skirt; when the inverness cape was set on their shoulders and the double-peaked cap was set on their heads; when men rode bicycles that could be mounted only if one had the spring of a leopard; when Madame Patti sang *Home, Sweet Home* under the gas-light glitter, and when Sherlock Holmes stole through the streets to solve some mystery; time of the transformation scene and the harlequinade, of roses from Picardy, and the Martini-Henry rifle; with two old children enjoying it all; a joyous jingling hour of life; a big, red berry on life's tree. A joy-ride: the pair of them were young again, and heaven was all around them.

James Kirke Paulding

A Southern Lady Delights in the City

from *New Mirror for Travellers; and Guide to the Springs*
1828

I could live in New York forever. We have a charming suit of rooms fronting on Broadway, that would be a perfect Paradise, were it not for the noise which prevents one's hearing oneself speak, and the dust which prevents one's seeing. But still it *is* delightful to sit at the window with a Waverley, and see the moving world forever passing to and fro, with unceasing footsteps. Every body appears to be in motion, and every thing else. The carriages rattle through the streets; the carts dance as if they were running races with them; the ladies trip along in all the colours of the rainbow; and the gentlemen look as though they actually had something to do. They all walk as if they were in a hurry, and on my remarking this to my uncle, he replied in his usual sarcastic manner, "Yes, they all seem as if they were running away from an indictment." I did not comprehend what he meant.

COMMUTER

Commuter—one who spends his life
In riding to and from his wife;
A man who shaves and takes a train
And then rides back to shave again.

E. B. White
from *The Lady Is Cold*
1946

C. THUSTRUP

Stephen Crane

Transformed Boulevard

New York's Bicycle Speedway; from the New York *Sun*,
July 5, 1896

The Bowery has had its day as a famous New York street. It is now a
mere tradition. Broadway will long hold its place as the chief vein
of the city's life. No process of expansion can ever leave it abandoned to the cheap clothing dealers and dime museum robbers. It
is too strategic in position. But lately the Western Boulevard
which slants from the Columbus monument at the southwest corner of Central Park to the river has vaulted to a startling promi-
nence and is now one of the sights of New York. This is caused by
the bicycle. Once the Boulevard was a quiet avenue whose particular distinctions were its shade trees and its third foot-walk which
extended in Parisian fashion down the middle of the street. Also it
was noted for its billboards and its huge and slumberous apartment
hotels. Now, however, it is the great thoroughfare for bicycles.
On these gorgeous spring days they appear in thousands. All mankind is a-wheel apparently and a person on nothing but legs feels
like a strange animal. A mighty army of wheels streams from the
brick wilderness below Central Park and speeds over the asphalt.
In the cool of the evening it returns with swaying and flashing of
myriad lamps.

The bicycle crowd has completely subjugated the street. The
glittering wheels dominate it from end to end. The cafes and dining rooms or the apartment hotels are occupied mainly by people
in bicycle clothes. Even the billboards have surrendered. They
advertise wheels and lamps and tires and patent saddles with all
the flaming vehemence of circus art. Even when they do conde-
scend to still advertise a patent medicine, you are sure to confront
a lithograph of a young person in bloomers who is saying in large
type: "Yes, George, I find that Willowrum always refreshes me
after these long rides."

Down at the Circle where stands the patient Columbus, the
stores are crowded with bicycle goods. There are innumerable
repair shops. Everything is bicycle. In the afternoon the parade
begins. The great discoverer, erect on his tall grey shaft, must feel
his stone head whirl when the battalions come swinging and shining around the curve.

It is interesting to note the way in which the blasphemous and
terrible truck-drivers of the lower part of the city will hunt a
bicyclist. A truck-driver, of course, believes that a wheelman is a
pest. The average man could not feel more annoyance if nature
had suddenly invented some new kind of mosquito. And so the
truck-driver resolves in his dreadful way to make life as troublous
and thrilling for the wheelman as he possibly can. The wheelman
suffers under a great handicap. He is struggling over the most
uneven cobbles which bless a metropolis. Twenty horses threaten
him and forty wheels miss his shoulder by an inch. In his ears there
is a hideous din. It surrounds him, envelopes him.

Add to this trouble, then, a truckman with a fiend's desire to see dead wheelmen. The situation affords deep excitement for everyone concerned.

But when a truck-driver comes to the Boulevard the beautiful balance of the universe is apparent. The teamster sits mute, motionless, casting sidelong glances at the wheels which spin by him. He still contrives to exhibit a sort of a sombre defiance, but he has no oath nor gesture nor wily scheme to drive a 3 ton wagon over the prostrate body of some unhappy cyclist. On the Boulevard this roaring lion from down town is so subdued, so isolated that he brings tears to the sympathetic eye.

There is a new game on the Boulevard. It is the game of Bicycle Cop and Scorcher. When the scorcher scorches beyond the patience of the law, the bicycle policeman, if in sight, takes after him. Usually the scorcher has a blissful confidence in his ability to scorch and thinks it much easier to just ride away from the policeman than to go to court and pay a fine. So they go flying up the Boulevard with the whole mob of wheelmen and wheelwomen, eager to see the race, sweeping after them. But the bicycle police are mighty hard riders and it takes a flier to escape them. The affair usually ends in calamity for the scorcher, but in the meantime fifty or sixty cyclists have had a period of delirious joy.

Bicycle Cop and Scorcher is a good game, but after all it is not as good as the game that was played in the old days when the suggestion of a corps of bicycle police in neat knickerbockers would have scandalized Mulberry street. This was the game of Fat Policeman on Foot Trying to Stop a Spurt. A huge, unwieldy officer rushing out into the street and wildly trying to head off and grab some rider who was spinning along in just one silver flash was a sight that caused the populace to turn out in a body. If some madman started at a fierce gait from the Columbus monument, he could have the consciousness that at frequent and exciting intervals, red-faced policemen would gallop out at him and frenziedly clutch at his coat-tails. And owing to a curious dispensation, the majority of the policemen along the boulevard were very stout and could swear most graphically in from two to five languages.

But they changed all that. The un-police-like bicycle police are wonderfully clever and the vivid excitement of other days is gone. Even the scorcher seems to feel depressed and narrowly looks over the nearest officer before he starts on his frantic career.

The girl in bloomers is, of course, upon her native heath when she steers her steel steed into the Boulevard. One becomes conscious of a bewildering variety in bloomers. There are some that fit and some that do not fit. There are some that were not made to fit and there are some that couldn't fit anyhow. As a matter of fact the bloomer costume is now in one of the primary stages of its evolution. Let us hope so at any rate. Of course every decent citizen concedes that women shall wear what they please and it is supposed that he convenants with himself not to grin and nudge his neighbor when anything particularly amazing passes him on the street but resolves to simply and industriously mind his own affairs. Still the situation no doubt harrows him greatly. No man was ever found to defend bloomers. His farthest statement, as an individual, is to advocate them for all women he does not know and cares nothing about. Most women become radical enough to say: "Why shouldn't I wear 'em, if I choose." Still, a second look at the Boulevard convinces one that the world is slowly, solemnly, inevitably coming to bloomers. We are about to enter an age of bloomers, and the bicycle, that machine which has gained an economic position of the most tremendous importance, is going to be responsible for more than the bruises on the departed fat policemen of the Boulevard.

Elizabeth Oates Smith
A Jam in Broadway
1854

There is no getting up nor down the street. There is a dead calm. The stage drivers compose themselves upon their boxes, assured of ten minutes of leisure. They crack jokes and whips at each other. Draymen plant themselves bolt upright, and relieve themselves by swearing. Porters change their burdens from side to side, but needing all their strength to carry them, do not swear. Handcarts are jammed up between drays and stages, and their holders now take the strap which they carry across their foreheads to help the draft, from its place, and hold up their heads to look about them. Boys are in ecstasies, running pell-mell in all directions, mounting upon stages, lamp-posts, and old awnings, everywhere that a boy can fix himself, (and where is the place upon which a boy cannot hang), and they shout and roar, and crack pea-nuts, and toss the shells upon the heads below, and think a Broadway jam the best fun in the world. One perfect little yahoo mounted upon a railing, spits upon the hats below with utter contempt for all decencies.

Passengers thread in and out amid this Babel with wondrous dexterity, now seizing the tongue of a stage, now ducking under the teeth of a horse, mounting a cart, doubling a wheel, zigzagging amid vehicles of every kind, composedly nonchalant of all the uproar. At length far down, a mile off, somewhere at the Bowling Green, the jam breaks, and the whole mass gives way. Presto! all is in motion, helter skelter—boys scamper like mad, drivers spur up, drays rattle and thump, newsboys begin to scream, cartmen buckle the belt to the brow and drop their heads like beasts of burden— whip, swear, whip, crack, scream, laugh, hurra—and all is in motion again.

Ogden Nash
What Street Is This, Driver?
from *Good Intentions*
1942

Let this be my tardy farewell
To the erstwhile Sixth Avenue El.
Though no longer a native New Yorker
My aesthetic eye is a corker;
The El had a twelve-foot clearance
And I notice its disappearance.
New York was to many a kingdom
Where business or pleasure bringdom,
But I got there so seldom
To me 'twas Sixth Avenue Eldom.
It never got anyone downer
Than this timid out-of-towner;
It ran like an iron entrail
Midway 'twixt Penn and Grand Central;
It staggered column by column
From the Battery up to Harlem,
And no matter wherever went you
The Sixth Avenue El went too.
You'd be riding from Park to Madison
While leafing through Steele or Addison,

And fleeter than meter could tell
You'd be twisting under the El;
Be you headed south or north
On Lexington, Park or Fourth
Any whither you wished to flit,
Lay the El between you and it.
Farewell, O El, farewell;
I was once of your clientele.
Although I'm no longer Manhattanized
I'm glad that we met and fraternized.
I remember warmly enough
The journeys to Coogan's Bluff,
And the tingling tangling nerve
As we rattled round Suicide Curve;
You could tell by the chuckling sound
That the train was Giant bound.
There was Laughing Larry Doyle
In the days when oil was oil,
And later, when oil was fusel,
We hollered for Emil Meusel.
McGeehan wrote better than Shelley
In descriptions of Long George Kelly;
Hoyt was adroit and hot
And Ott a promising tot,
And I'd rather have met Frankie Frisch
Than marry Lillian Gish;
To win was the only law
And the law was John McGraw.
Ah, then we placed our reliance
On the El and on the Giants;
Now the El with McGraw is buried,
And the torrid Giants are terried,
Now realtors along Sixth Avenue
Anticipate mounting revenue.
No more the El careens
Past intimate family scenes;
Housewives no longer gape
From window and fire escape
At passengers packed like pemmican
Who are gaping back at them again;
Like Wichita, or Los Angeles,
Sixth Ave. is now new-fangelous,
Light as an air by Bizet,
And broad as the Champs Elysées.
Fit for Geddes (Norman Bel)
Is Sixth Avenue minus the El.
This notable civic improvement
Facilitates traffic movement;
It clears the street for sleighs
And the sidewalks for cafés.
O El, thy era is o'er;
I am glad that thou art no more;
But I'd hold myself lower than dirt
Weren't I glad that once thou wert.

ISAC FRIEDLANDER

SEYMOUR CHWAST

James Dickey

For the Running of the New York City Marathon

1979

If you would run

If you would quicken the city with your pelting,
　　Then line up, be counted, and change
　Your body into time, and with me through the boxed maze
　flee
　　　On soft hooves, saying　all saying in flock-breath
　　　Take me there.
　　　　　　　　　　I am against you
　　　　　And with you:　I am second
Wind and native muscle in the streets　my image lost and
　discovered
　Among yours:　lost and found in the endless panes
　　　Of a many-gestured bald-headed woman, caught between
　One set of clothes and tomorrow's:　naked, pleading in her
　wax
　　　　For the right, silent words to praise
　　　　The herd-hammering pulse of our sneakers,
　　And the time gone by when we paced
River-sided, close-packed in our jostled beginning,
　　O my multitudes.　We are streaming from the many
　　　to the one

At a time, our ghosts chopped-up by the windows
Of merchants;　the mirroring store-fronts let us, this one day,
　　　Wear on our heads feet and backs
　What we would wish.　This day I have taken in my stride
　　　Swank jogging-suits rayed with bright emblems
　Too good for me:　have worn in blood-sweating weather
　Blizzard-blind parkas and mukluks, a lightning-struck hairpiece
　　　Or two, and the plumes of displayed Zulu chieftains.

Through the colors of day I move as one must move
　　　His shadow somewhere on
Farther into the dark.　Any hour now　any minute
　　　Attend the last rites
　　　Of pure plod-balance!　Smoke of the sacrificial
Olympic lamb in the Deli!　O swooping and hairline-hanging
　　　Civic-minded placement of bridges!　Hallelujas of bars!
　　　　Teach those who have trained in the sunrise
　　　　On junk-food and pop, how to rest　how to rise
　From the timed city's never-die dead.　Through the
　　spattering echo
　Of Vulcanized hundreds, being given the finish-line
　　hot-foot,
　　　　I am lolloping through to the end,
　　By man-dressing mannequins clad　by flashes of sun
　　on squared rivers

As we breast our own breathless arrival:　as we home in,
　　　Ahead of me　me　and behind me
Winning over the squirrel-wheel's outlasted stillness, on the
　unearthly pull and fall
　　　Of our half-baked soles, all agony-smiles
　　　and all winning—

　　　　All winning, one after one.

My City

Piri Thomas
Down These Mean Streets
1967

In the daytime Harlem looks kinda dirty and the people a little drab and down. But at night, man, it's a swinging place, especially Spanish Harlem. The lights transform everything into life and movement and blend the different colors into a magic cover-all that makes the drabness and garbage, wailing kids and tired people invisible. Shoes and clothes that by day look beat and worn out, at night take on a reflected splendor that the blazing multi-colored lights burn on them. Everyone seems to develop a sense of urgent rhythm and you get the impression that you have to walk with a sense of timing.

The daytime pain fades alongside the feeling of belonging and just being in swing with all the humming kicks going on around you. I'd stand on a corner and close my eyes and look at everything through my nose. I'd sniff deep and see the *cuchifritos* and hot dogs, stale sweat and dried urine. I'd smell the worn-out mothers with six or seven kids, and the nonpatient fathers beating the hell out of them. My nose would get a high-pitch tingling from the gritty wailing and bouncing red light of a squad car passing the scene like a bat out of Harlem, going to cool some trouble, or maybe cause some.

I'd walk on Lexington Avenue, where a lot of things were going on, and hear the long, strung-out voice of a junkie, "Hey, man, you got a couple charlies you can lend me?"...

I'd meet my boys, and all the other hearing and seeing suddenly became unimportant. Only my boys were the important kick, and for good reasons—if I had boys, I had respect and no other clique would make me open game. Besides, they gave me a feeling of belonging, of prestige, of accomplishment; I felt *grande* and bad. Sometimes the thoughts would start flapping around inside me about the three worlds I lived in—the world of home, the world of school (no more of that, though), and the world of street. The street was the best damn one. It was like all the guys shouting out, "Hey, man, this is our kick."

The worlds of home and school were made up of rules laid down by adults who had forgotten the feeling of what it means to be a kid but expected a kid to remember to be an adult—something he hadn't gotten to yet. The world of street belonged to the kid alone. There he could earn his own rights, prestige, his good-o stick of living. It was like being a knight of old, like being ten feet tall.

Avery Corman
The Old Neighborhood
1980

We lived in the Kingsbridge Road-Grand Concourse section of the Bronx in a red brick building on Morris Avenue. Flamingos caroused on the wallpaper in the lobby and art deco nymphs were painted on the elevator door of "Beatrice Arms," named for the landlord's wife, Beatrice. The building's most distinguished citizen was The Dentist, who had an office on the ground floor, the smell of ether lingered in the lobby.

My best friends were Arthur Pollack and Jerry Rosen....

Jerry lived in my building, his father was Rosen's Dry Cleaning on Kingsbridge Road. Arthur was the rich one among us, his father worked in Manhattan for a printing company, and Arthur owned electric baseball. We were Yankee fans, my favorite player was George "Snuffy" Stirnweiss, who led the American League in batting in 1945 with a wartime average of .309. His picture was pasted to the wall above my bed, along with my collection of Dixie Cup covers with scenes of "Our Branches of Service in Action." I listened to Yankee games on the radio, the road games re-created

ROBERT ANDREW PARKER

MIGUEL COVARRUBIAS

STEVEN LACK

in the studio to the sound of the Western Union ticker: "Grimes hits a high fly"...tick...tick...tick..."It's down the left field line"...tick... tick..."It's"...tick...tick...tick...tick.... "A foul ball." Time was suspended in these reports, which came in from such exotic places as Cleveland and Chicago.

My parents, Sylvia and Bernard Robbins, had moved to this neighborhood from the Lower East Side the year I was born. They came north by subway to a new social position in their lives, to an area with parks and elevator buildings. My father had been hired as an assistant manager of a men's haberdashery store on Fordham Road. Six feet one with reddish hair, he was slightly stoop-shouldered, as if he were embarrassed to be taller than his neighbors. My mother was small and fair with fragile features, a woman who attempted to manage her responsibilities as she perceived them—to run the household and be informed. Our family and The Dentist and his wife were the only people in the building to read *The New York Times,* not held in high regard in the neighborhood, as it did not have horse-racing tips or the comics.

My father, 4-F because of a heart murmur, was an air-raid warden, out on the streets during blackouts. In his work, after ten years in the Bronx, he was still an assistant manager in the haberdashery, which meant that he was but a salesman entrusted to use the cash register. He was extremely low-keyed in business. The store manager told my mother, "He's too nice."

Angry with my father, my mother confronted him at the dinner table. "What salesman should be called nice? They should be saying you're aggressive!"

"Some of these salesmen—they'll sell you anything," he answered, defending himself, turning to me. "Even clothes that don't fit. I can't do that."

He did not advance in his work or earn the money that others did, but he was honest, the word in the neighborhood was that people respected him. So he was retained in his job by a succession of store managers he never replaced.

Our apartment was decorated modestly, bare wood floors, mahogany pieces, wing chairs and a greenish tweed couch in the living room. The prized piece was our push-button console radio, an Emerson, purchased on time. Some families in the neighborhood went to the Catskills or to Rockaway for the summer, as my mother was given to remind my father. On Sundays we went to Orchard Beach by bus. They argued often over money. I pretended not to listen. My mother never took a job to help the family income because in the neighborhood wives did not work, unless the husband was in the army or dead. Neither the husband nor the wife would have approved of the woman working. This was cultural, a given, in the same way that troubled couples, as my parents were, never got divorced. As I think back, thirty-five years later, remembering that besieged couple and the tired man who was my father, it is astonishing to me that I am an older man now than my father was then.

Alfred Kazin
A Walker in the City
1951

We were of the city, but somehow not in it. Whenever I went off on my favorite walk to Highland Park in the "American" district to the north, on the border of Queens, and climbed the hill to the old reservoir from which I could look straight across to the skyscrapers of Manhattan, I saw New York as a foreign city. There, brilliant and unreal, the city had its life, as Brownsville was ours. That the two were joined in me I never knew then—not even on those glorious summer nights of my last weeks in high school when, with what an ache, I would come back into Brownsville along Liberty Avenue, and, as soon as I could see blocks ahead of me the Labor Lyceum, the malted milk and Fatima signs over the candy stores, the old women in their housedresses sitting in front of the tenements like priestesses of an ancient cult, knew I was home.

We were the end of the line. We were the children of the immigrants who had camped at the city's back door, in New York's rawest, remotest, cheapest ghetto, enclosed on one side by the Carnarsie flats and on the other by the hallowed middle-class districts that showed the way to New York. "New York" was what we put last on our address, but first in thinking of the others around us. *They* were New York, the Gentiles, America; we were Brownsville—*Brunzvil,* as the old folks said—the dust of the earth to all Jews with money, and notoriously a place that measured all success by our skill in getting away from it. So that when poor Jews left, *even* Negroes, as we said, found it easy to settle on the margins of Brownsville, and with the coming of spring, bands of Gypsies, who would rent empty stores, hang their rugs around them like a desert tent, and bring a dusty and faintly sinister air of carnival into our neighborhood.

*   *   *

For all those first summer walks into the city, all daily walks across the bridge for years afterward, when I came to leave Brownsville at last, were efforts to understand one single half-hour at dusk, on a dark winter day, the year I was fourteen. There had been some school excursion that day to City Hall and the courts of lower New York, and looking up at the green dome of the *World* as we came into Park Row, I found myself separated from the class, and decided to go it across the bridge alone. I remember holding a little red volume of THE WORLD'S GREATEST SELECTED SHORT STORIES in my hand as I started out under the groined arcade of the Municipal Building and the rusty green-black terminal of the El sweeping Brooklyn Bridge. Suddenly I felt lost and happy as I went up another flight of steps, passed under the arches of the tower, and waited, next to a black barrel, at the railing of the observation platform. The trolleys clanged and clanged; every angry stalled car below sounded its horn as, bumper to bumper, they all poked their way along the bridge; the El trains crackled and thundered over my right shoulder. A clock across the street showed its lighted face; along the fire escapes of the building were sculptured figures of runners and baseball players, of prize fighters flexing their muscles and wearing their championship belts, just as they did in the *Police Gazette.* But from that platform under the tower the way ahead was strange. Only the electric sign of the Jewish Daily *Forward,* burning high over the tenements of the East Side, suddenly stilled the riot in my heart as I saw the cables leap up to the tower, saw those great meshed triangles leap up and up, higher and still higher—Lord my Lord, when will they cease to drive me up with them in their flight?—and then, each line singing out alone the higher it came and nearer, fly flaming into the topmost eyelets of the tower.

Somewhere below they were roasting coffee, handling spices—the odor was in the pillars, in the battered wooden planks of the promenade under my feet, in the blackness upwelling from the river. A painter's scaffold dangled down one side of the tower over a spattered canvas. Never again would I walk Brooklyn Bridge without smelling that coffee, those spices, the paint on that canvas. The trolley car clanged, clanged, clanged taking me home that day from the bridge. Papa, where are they taking me? Where in this beyond are they taking me?

Helen Keller
I Go Adventuring
1929

Cut off as I am, it is inevitable that I should sometimes feel like a shadow walking in a shadowy world. When this happens I ask to be taken to New York City. Always I return home weary but I have the comforting certainty that mankind is real flesh and I myself am not a dream.

EVERETT SHINN

there, venting their passions—struggling, kicking, and shuddering like marionettes. Ten minutes after he left the station, he saw a taxi driver kill a peddler in an argument over who had the right of way on an empty street. He wanted no part of this city. It was too gray, cold, and dangerous. It was perhaps the grayest, coldest, most dangerous city in the world. He understood why young people from all over came to pit themselves against it. But he was too old for such things, and he had already been to war.

F. Scott Fitzgerald
My Lost City
1932

From the ruins, lonely and inexplicable as the sphinx, rose the Empire State Building and, just as it had been a tradition of mine to climb to the Plaza Roof to take leave of the beautiful city, extending as far as eyes could reach, so now I went to the roof of the last and most magnificent of towers. Then I understood—everything was explained: I had discovered the crowning error of the city, its Pandora's box. Full of vaunting pride the New Yorker had climbed here and seen with dismay what he had never suspected, that the city was not the endless succession of canyons that he had supposed but that *it had limits*—from the tallest structure he saw for the first time that it faded out into the country on all sides, into an expanse of green and blue that alone was limitless. . . .

ROBERT NEUBECKER

Mark Helprin
A Winter's Tale
1983

The day that Hardesty arrived in New York was cold and dry. Nevertheless, tentative whirlwinds of snow sometimes swept the avenues, twisting about in gray light. The city had not yet been interred in its January shroud, and the fact that the streets were still bare gave December the air of fall, just as reluctant snowbanks can give the air of December even to May.

This was the first city he had ever seen that immediately spoke for itself, as if it had no people and were a system of empty canyons cutting across the desert in the west. The overwhelming mass of its architecture, in which time crossed and mixed, did not ask for attention shyly, like Paris or Copenhagen, but demanded it like a centurion barking orders. Great plumes of steam a hundred stories tall, river traffic that ran a race to silver bays, and countless thousands of intersecting streets that sometimes would break away from the grid and soar over the rivers on the flight path of a high bridge, were merely the external signs of something deeper that was straining hard to be.

Hardesty knew right off that an unseen force was breathing under all the gray, that the events and miracles of the city were simply the effect of this force as it turned in its sleep, that it saturated everything, and that it had sculpted the city before it had even opened its eyes. He felt it striving in everything he saw, and knew that the entire population, though prideful of its independence, was subject to a complete and intense orchestration the likes of which he had never imagined. They rushed about here and

AMERICA, AMERICA!

I am a poet of the Hudson River and the heights above it,
    the lights, the stars, and the bridges
I am also by self-appointment the laureate of the Atlantic
    —of the peoples' hearts, crossing it
      to new America.

I am burdened with the truck and chimera, hope,
    acquired in the sweating sick-excited passage
      in steerage, strange and estranged
Hence I must descry and describe the kingdom of emotion.

For I am a poet of the kindergarten (in the city)
    and the cemetery (in the city)
And rapture and ragtime and also the secret city in the heart and
    mind.
This is the song of the natural city self in the 20th century.

It is true but only partly true that a city is a "tyranny of numbers"
(This is the chant of the urban metropolitan and metaphysical self
After the first two World Wars of the 20th century)

—This is the city self, looking from window to lighted window
When the squares and checks of faintly yellow light
Shine at night, upon a huge dim board and slab-like tombs,
Hiding many lives. It is the city consciousness
Which sees and says: more: more and more: always more.

Delmore Schwartz
1954

EUGENE MIHAESCO

HOWARD COOK

Bernard G. Richards

My Vacation on the East Side

from *Discourses of Keidansky*
1903

HANS ALEXANDER MUELLER

"Green fields, fair forests, singing streams, pine-clad mountains, verdant vistas—from the monotony of the city to the monotony of nature. I wanted a complete change, and so I went to the East Side of New York for my vacation. That is where I have been."

Thus did our friend explain his strange disappearance and unusual absence from Boston for a whole week. For the first time since he came here from New York he had been missing from his home, his regular haunts, such as the cafés, Jewish book-stores and the debating club, and none of those whom I asked knew whither he had betaken himself. The direct cause of his disappearance, explained Keidansky, was a railroad pass, which he had secured from a friendly editor for whom he had done some work. He went on explaining. "I wanted to break away for a while from the sameness and solemnness, the routine and respectability of this town, from my weary idleness, empty labors, and uniformity of our ideas here, so when the opportunity was available I took a little journey to the big metropolis. One becomes rusty and falls into a rut in this suburb. I was becoming so sedate, stale and quiet that I was beginning to be afraid of myself. The revolutionary spirit has somewhat subsided. Many of the comrades have gone back on their ideas, have begun to practise what they preach, to improve their conditions by going into business and into work, and I often feel lonely. Anti-imperialism, Christian Science and the New Thought are amusing; but there is not enough excitement here. Boston is not progressive; there are not enough foreigners in this city. People from many lands with all sorts of ideas and the friction that arises between them—that causes progress. New York is the place, and it is also the refuge of all radicals, revolutionaries, and good people whom the wicked old world has cast out. America, to retain its original character, must constantly be replenished by hounded refugees and victims of persecution in despotic lands. To remain lovers of freedom we must have sufferers from oppression with us. Sad commentary, this, upon our human nature; but so are nearly all commentaries upon human nature. Commentaries upon the superhuman are tragic. New York with its Germans and Russians and Jews is a characteristic American city. Boston and other places are too much like Europe—cold, narrow and provincial. I came to Boston some time ago because I had relatives here—the last reason in the world why any one should go anywhere; but I was ignorant and superstitious in those days. I have since managed to emancipate myself, more or less, from the baneful influences of those near; but meanwhile I have established myself, have become interested in the movements and institutions of the community, and here I am. The symphony concerts, the radical movement, the library, lectures on art, the sunsets over the Charles River, the Faneuil Hall protest meetings against everything that continues to be, the literary paper published, the Atlantic Monthly, Gamaliel Bradford, Philip Hale and so many other fixtures of Boston have since endeared it to me and I stayed. Besides, it would cost me too much to ship all my books to New York. . . . But this time I wanted a complete change; I wanted something to move and stir me out of the given groove, the beaten path I was falling into, some excitement that would shake the cobwebs out of my brain, so I turned towards the East Side.

"They are all there, the comrades, the radicals, the red ones, and dreamers; people who are free because they own nothing. Poets, philosophers, novelists, dramatists, artists, editors, agitators, and other idle and useless beings, they form a great galaxy in the New York Ghetto. For several years, ever since I left New York, I had been receiving instruction and inspiration from them through the medium of the Yiddish and the Socialist press, where my own things often appeared beside their spirited outpourings, and now I was overcome by an overpowering desire to meet them again, talk matters over and fight it all out. There is no sham about the East Side branch of the ancient and most honorable order of Bohemians—the little changing, moving world that is flowing with the milk of human kindness and the honey of fraternal affections, where those who live may die and those who die may live. Here among the East Side Bohemians people feel freely, act independently, speak as they think and are not at all ashamed of their feelings. They have courage. They wear their convictions in public. They do as they please, whether that pleases everybody else or not. They talk with the purpose of saying something. They write with the object of expressing their ideas. They tell the truth and shame those who do not. Hearts are warm because they own their souls. Those who really own their souls will never lose them. . . .

"I cannot tell you more, but these meetings and these talks at various times and in various places made my vacation on the East Side delightful. Then there were lectures and meetings and social gatherings of the comrades. The sun of new ideas rises on the East Side. Everywhere you meet people who are ready to fight for what they believe in and who do not believe in fighting. For a complete change and for pure air you must go among the people who think about something, have faith in something. Katz, Cahan, Gordin, Yanofsky, Zolotaroff, Harkavy, Frumkin, Krantz, Zametkin, Zeifert, Lessin, Elisovitz, Winchevsky, Jeff, Leontief, Lipsky, Freidus, Frominson, Selikowitch, Palay, Barondess, and many other intellectual leaders, come into the cafés to pour out wisdom and drink tea, and here comes also Hutchins Hapgood to get his education. Each man bears his own particular lantern, it is true, but each one carries a light and every one brings a man with him. . . .

"Why," added Keidansky, as a final thunderbolt, "I have gained enough ideas on the East Side to last me here in Boston for ten years."

Charles G. Shaw
Night Life
1931

In all the world I know no city offering the nocturnal diversion to be had in New York. I believe this metropolis to be wider open now than ever before. I have found that rainy nights, nine times in ten, make more for adventure than fine ones. I believe that N. T. Granlund is the town's best floor show stager and the Messrs. O'Keefe and Joe Lewis the top ceremonial masters. I regard Texas Guinan as the Queen of all night clubs.

I deplore the Yorkville trick of forcing you to sit with strangers, even though the room be filled with empty tables. I cannot help feeling that nearly all orchestras play twice as loudly as they should. I consider Charlie Journal a perfect maitre d'hotel and regret the passing of the Club Montmartre more than words can tell. I know of few taxi drivers possessing the courtesy of James Rivais, whose license is 51742 and whose hangout is Jungle Alley.

I am fetched by the offerings of Hubert's Museum but can say nothing in praise of Sixth Avenue's penny peep-shows. I am always filled with memories when visiting the Cafe des Beaux Arts. I believe that Lee "Harlemania" Posner knows his Harlem as no other white man. I believe the minimum check will, in time, supplant the cover charge.

I consider the Central Park Casino a breathtaking piece of decor. I believe that New York boasts almost as many great food halls as Paris. I know of no single first rate night club that graces upper Broadway.

I often wonder what has happened to Walter Sweeney who ran the Cohasset Club. I like the comfort of Luchow's with its excellent German fare, the pace of the Hollywood's floor show, and the chicken at Tillie's Inn. I believe that nine times out of ten, the better the band, the worse the food.

I do not believe that the town to-day offers an equal to Jack's Oyster House. I am convinced that the Irish make the best waiters, the French the best chefs, the Italians the best bootleggers.

I believe that a night club's most exciting hours are between 1:00 and 3 A.M. I am pleased by the vast improvement in liquor during the past six months. I have usually found the gayest exteriors to harbour the dullest hangouts.

I do not believe there has ever been a cafe-bar equal to Forty-fourth Street Sherry's. I know few orchestras in any land that compare with Emil Coleman's, Leo Reisman's, or Guy Lombardo's. I pin the blue ribbon for flower girls on Mavis King of the late Argonaut. I believe that the next change in night life will centre around the dance.

I consider Broadway fully as diverting as Montmartre. I believe

that where one innovation clicks, over a hundred flop. I deplore the passing of Maennerchor Hall that once graced East Fifty-sixth Street.

I believe that from 1911 to 1915 New York hit its top night stride. I prefer a sawdust-floored saloon to a batik-curtained tea-room. I believe the Provincetown Playhouse to be the town's most uncomfortable theatre. I am sorry that the bronze owls that winked their electric-lighted eyes on the Herald Building are no more.

I consider more than four cocktails before dinner excessive. I regard dancing without some kind of heart interest as the near-beer of diversion. I am unable to appreciate the charm of any open-faced restaurant. I prefer Italian to German opera and silent films to the talkies.

I do not like the foyer of the Forrest Theatre, the pretentiousness of Reuben's, cocktails containing absinthe, and the bouncer at the Club Elite. I prefer the Colony Restaurant's entrees to the majority of its patrons. I regret that Columbus Avenue's Old Landmark isn't what it used to be.

I consider the burning of the Sherry-Netherland tower New York's most artistic fire. I have never witnessed anything worth a cent at the Cherry Lane Theatre. I admire the divan seats at the Capitol. I don't think there is any such thing as an "average taxi driver."

I believe Manhattan night life to be gayer than that of London, less genuine than Berlin's, and more amusing than that of Paris. I believe that whether there be speakeasies or not New York will always have night clubs. I regret that some of the spots mentioned in this book have probably gone out of business.

Henry David Thoreau
Letter to R. W. Emerson
1843

You must not count much upon what I can do or learn in New York. I feel a good way off here; and it is not to be visited, but seen and dwelt in. I have been there but once, and have been confined to the house since. Everything there disappoints me but the crowd; rather, I was disappointed with the rest before I came. I have no eyes for their churches, and what else they find to brag of. Though I know but little about Boston, yet what attracts me, in a quiet way, seems much meaner and more pretending than there,—libraries, pictures, and faces in the street. You don't know where any respectability inhabits. It is in the crowd in Chatham Street. The crowd is something new, and to be attended to. It is worth a thousand Trinity Churches and Exchanges while it is looking at them, and will run over them and trample them under foot one day. There are two things I hear and am aware I live in the neighborhood of,—the roar of the sea and the hum of the city. . . .

I don't like the city better, the more I see it, but worse. I am ashamed of my eyes that behold it. It is a thousand times meaner than I could have imagined. It will be something to hate,—that's the advantage it will be to me; and even the best people in it are a part of it, and talk coolly about it. The pigs in the street are the most respectable part of the population. When will the world learn that a million men are of no importance compared with *one* man? But I must wait for a shower of shillings, or at least a slight dew or mizzling of sixpences, before I explore New York very far.

PHILIPPE WEISBECKER

VILLAGE REVISITED

(*A cheerful lament in which truth, pain, and beauty are prominently mentioned, and in that order*)

In the days of my youth, in the days of my youth,
I lay in West Twelfth Street, writhing with Truth.
I died in Jones Street, dallying with pain,
And flashed up Sixth Avenue, risen again.

In the terrible beautiful age of my prime,
I lacked for sweet linen but never for time.
The tree in the alley was potted in gold,
The girls on the buses would never grow old.

Last night with my love I returned to these haunts
To visit Pain's diggings and try for Truth's glance;
I was eager and ardent and waited as always
The answering click to my ring in the hallways,
But Truth hardly knew me, and Pain wasn't in
(It scarcely seemed possible Pain wasn't in).

Beauty recalled me. We bowed in the Square,
In the wonderful westerly Waverly air.
She had a new do, I observed, to her hair.

E. B. White
1944

Michael Gold

Jews Without Money

1930

I can never forget the East Side street where I lived as a boy.

It was a block from the notorious Bowery, a tenement canyon hung with fire-escapes, bed-clothing, and faces.

Always these faces at the tenement windows. The street never failed them. It was an immense excitement. It never slept. It roared like a sea. It exploded like fireworks.

People pushed and wrangled in the street. There were armies of howling pushcart peddlers. Women screamed, dogs barked and copulated. Babies cried.

A parrot cursed. Ragged kids played under truck-horses. Fat housewives fought from stoop to stoop. A beggar sang.

At the livery stable coach drivers lounged on a bench. They hee-hawed with laughter, they guzzled cans of beer.

Pimps, gamblers and red-nosed bums; peanut politicians, pugilists in sweaters; tinhorn sports and tall longshoremen in overalls. An endless pageant of East Side life passed through the wicker doors of Jake Wolf's saloon.

The saloon goat lay on the sidewalk, and dreamily consumed a *Police Gazette*.

East Side mothers with heroic bosoms pushed their baby carriages, gossiping. Horse cars jingled by. A tinker hammered at brass. Junkbells clanged.

Whirlwinds of dust and newspaper. The prostitutes laughed shrilly. A prophet passed, an old-clothes Jew with a white beard. Kids were dancing around the hurdy-gurdy. Two bums slugged each other.

Excitement, dirt, fighting, chaos! The sound of my street lifted like the blast of a great carnival or catastrophe. The noise was always in my ears. Even in sleep I could hear it; I can hear it now.

James Baldwin

Go Tell It on the Mountain

1954

He left Fifth Avenue and walked west towards the movie houses. Here on 42nd Street it was less elegant but no less strange. He loved this street, not for the people or the shops but for the stone lions that guarded the great main building of the Public Library, a building filled with books and unimaginably vast, and which he had never yet dared to enter. He might, he knew, for he was a member of the branch in Harlem and was entitled to take books from any library in the city. But he had never gone in because the building was so big that it must be full of corridors and marble steps, in the maze of which he would be lost and never find the book he wanted. And then everyone, all the white people inside would know that he was not used to great buildings, or to many books, and they would look at him with pity. He would enter on another day, when he had read all the books uptown, an achievement that would, he felt, lend him the poise to enter any building in the world.

HENRIK DRESCHER

Marianne Moore

New York

1935

the savage's romance,
accreted where we need the space for commerce—
the centre of the wholesale fur trade,
starred with tepees of ermine and peopled with foxes,
the long guard-hairs waving two inches beyond the body of the
   pelt;
the ground dotted with deer-skins—white with white spots,
'as satin needlework in a single colour may carry a varied
   pattern',
and wilting eagle's-down compacted by the wind;
and picardels of beaver-skin; white ones alert with snow.
It is a far cry from the 'queen full of jewels'
and the beau with the muff,
from the gilt coach shaped like a perfume-bottle,
to the conjunction of the Monongahela and the Allegheny,
and the scholastic philosophy of the wilderness
to combat which one must stand outside and laugh
since to go in is to be lost.
It is not the dime-novel exterior,
Niagara Falls, the calico horses and the war-canoe;
it is not that 'if the fur is not finer than such as one sees others
   wear,
one would rather be without it'—
that estimated in raw meat and berries, we could feed the
   universe;
it is not the atmosphere of ingenuity,
the otter, the beaver, the puma skins
without shooting-irons or dogs;
it is not the plunder,
but 'accessibility to experience.'

Lewis Mumford
New York Realists
from *The New Yorker*, 1937

The other day, while I was prowling through the exhibition of the New York realists at the Whitney Museum—it was not the critics' preview—I became suddenly conscious of the other visitors. They were the sort of people you might expect to find at a fire, but never at an art gallery. There were groups of crisp, black-haired men, with cheeks like Westphalian hams, whom you might see dining at Cavanagh's or at Joe's in Brooklyn; there were shrewd horsey-faced fellows you'd more likely meet in the paddocks or the prize ring, judging limbs and shoulders, than in the midst of a collection of paintings. Politicians, real-estate brokers, contractors, lawyers —what were they doing here? My guess is that they were New Yorkers, pulled into the gallery by that dark, secret love for the city that New Yorkers hide from the world even when they brag about the city's wonders. And they had come to the right place, for the nine artists who are represented in this show,* through the work they did between 1900 and 1914, loved the city too; not less, per-

haps, because five of them came from the dingy, unexciting provincial streets of Philadelphia as it was at the beginning of the century.

To their contemporaries these artists were tough babies. Four of them had got their training after art school doing sketches for the Philadelphia Press, and they all had the journalist's eye for news and human interest, and they weren't afraid of going off the old beats to find them. There had been genre painters of New York life before: men like J. G. Brown, who had painted bootblacks and gamins. But these figures had no more aesthetic importance than a Horatio Alger hero, whose precise counterpart they, in fact, were. When Luks caught two little urchins dancing wildly, he didn't bother to change their clothes or wash their faces; he slashed their figures onto the canvas with a vigor begotten of his own delight. When in the 'Wake of the Ferry,' Sloan shows a lonely figure of a woman, standing partly exposed to the rain, looking out over the gray waters, he symbolizes forever the intense loneliness, as final as that of a deserted hermit on a Himalayan peak, almost everyone has known in the midst of crowded Manhattan.

*Henri, Luks, Sloan, Glackens, Bellows, Coleman, Lawson, Shinn, and Du Bois.

ANDREZJ CZECOT

PETER SIS

FORTY-TWO WASHINGTON SQUARE

In winter the water is frigid,
In summer the water is hot;
And we're forming a club for controlling the tub
For there's only one bath to the lot.
You shave in unlathering Croton,
If there's water at all, which is rare—
But the life isn't bad for a talented lad
At Forty-two Washington Square!

The dust it flies in at the window,
The smells they come in at the door,
Our trousers lie meek where we threw 'em last week
Bestrewing the maculate floor.
The gas isn't all that it should be,
It flickers—and yet I declare
There's pleasure or near it for young men of spirit
At Forty-two Washington Square!

But nobody questions your morals,
And nobody asks for the rent—
There's no one to pry if we're tight, you and I,
Or demand how our evenings are spent.
The furniture's ancient but plenty,
The linen is spotless and fair,
O life is a joy to a broth of a boy
At Forty-two Washington Square!

John Reed
from *The Day in Bohemia*
1913

Joyce Kilmer

Incongruous New York

1916

The dwellers in a great European city would give their proudest avenue of great shops and rich clubs some dignified and significant title, like the Rue de la Paix or the Friedrichstrasse. The Asiatics would give it a name more definitely descriptive and laudatory, like "The Street of the Thousand and One Mirrors of Delight." The New Yorkers, "laconic and Olympian," designate it by a simple numeral. They call it Fifth Avenue.

It comes partly from the national reticence, this prosaic name of a poetic thoroughfare. It is a manifestation of that attitude of mind which makes us to call a venerated and beloved statesman merely "Old Abe," when the English would call him "the Grand Old Man" and the Italians "the Star-crowned Patriarch." Also it is a phase of our democracy. We will not seem to exalt one avenue over another by giving it a fairer name; Fifth Avenue sounds to the uninitiated no more wealthy and aristocratic than Fourth Avenue. Indeed, if there be any partiality in the awarding of names, it would seem to be exercised in favor of First Avenue or Avenue A.

It may be objected that the sponsors of Fifth Avenue did not foresee its destined splendor. But this fact does not alter the case; we continue to call it Fifth Avenue, whereas Europeans would alter its name to something more appropriate to its grandeur. . . .

To give a street of wonders an austere name, to build palaces and fill them with offices and shops—these are the acts by which Americans are known. And especially does the New Yorker delight in the whimsical, the inconsistent, the unexpected. He is like a child who likes to dig in the sand with a silver spoon and to eat porridge with a toy shovel.

And this delicate perversity has its refreshing aspect. Fifth Avenue, surely, is a thing to admire in the new sense as well as the old. It sometimes suggests, perhaps, the ill-natured definition of a New Yorker as a man who, when he makes a set of chimes, puts it in a life insurance building. But it more often suggests a restatement of this definition; that is, that a New Yorker is a man who, when he makes a life insurance building, puts a set of chimes in it. . . .

But most of New York's romantic places get their glory not by plan, but by the accident of design. You turn the corner from a sombre street lined by tall concrete and steel structures that obviously are of your own period and come suddenly upon a mellow bit of New Amsterdam. You would not be surprised to see old Peter Stuyvesant stump down Coenties Slip and drop in for his morning's Hollands at "22½," across the way. There are streets and squares and alleys in downtown New York that look now exactly as they did when Times Square was a cow pasture and the Bowery really bowery. But these places were not romantic to the citizens of that time; they would not be romantic to us if by some strange backward transmigration of souls we should inhabit a vanished century.

No, we are fortunate to live when Battery Place and Coenties Slip have acquired romance's glamour. Incongruity is the soul of romance. And these quaint time-hallowed places have the loveliest sort of incongruity—the magical incongruity of archaisms.

Kate Simon

Battles and Celebrations

1982

In the fall, shapes became brisk, as sharp as the folds on new book covers. The hat factory smoke gathered itself together like long horses to ride the wind. The pale, weak forearms of our summer fathers disappeared under stiff dark cloth. Buildings began again to look like precise cutouts. The leaves fell from my tree and dried and turned in the gutter, making sounds like funeral veils. The jingling wagon of the ices man and its colored bottles disappeared. The icebox iceman put on his wool beanie with the pompom. Mrs. Katz closed the front window of her candy store and one could no longer buy from the sidewalk or hang out there as if one were going to buy, any minute. The gardeners in Crotona Park pulled out the red spikey flowers and gave them to us in big bunches. The *goyish* butchers hung the gray stretched-out bodies of hares in their windows. The kosher butchers heaped mounds of chicken fat to be rendered for use in Rosh Hashanah meals that celebrated the Hebrew New Year. Warm-skinned fruits gave way to cool apples and round purple Concord grapes appeared in slatted baskets in every greenstore, and Jews and Italians on the block began to make wine. In a corner of every kitchen was a purple mess to which sugar was added and, I think, alcohol; it was watched and fed, attended to as if each family had a new baby. And, like a monstrous new baby, the wine stank up the street; it was a fleshy acrid smell, dark and dusty, and the end product that we sipped never seemed worth the trouble, the worried care. (Was I jealous of a small vat of spoiled grapes? Quite possibly. At times there seemed to be no limit to the greed for feeling jealous.)

Among the fall fashions that swept in on us from inventive Arthur Avenue, like making rings of dried peach pits, decorating the backs of our hands with cockamamies, soaking bubble gum in a glass of water overnight—as Joey's father did his false teeth—to make it hard and resistantly chewy the next morning, was that of embroidering, part of a *Little Women* phase, a time of maidenly dignity and refinement. We girls had small embroidery hoops, a few hanks of colored thread, and a stamped bit of cloth to work on. In for the sociability rather than the craft, a number of us settled for fast cross-stitching. When confronted with a leaf or flower, some would make a loop, catch it with a stitch at the end, and there it was, a petal. Those of us who, like myself, came from houses of dexterous, admired hands filled in the leaves and petals laboriously and with satisfaction as the spaces became shape and color, the cloth stippled with French knots and its edges tastefully tassled.

Ranged at the sides of the stoop stairs, six or eight of us sat like Old Country village women tatting or knitting in gossiping twilights. We let the gossiping go and sang and sang even when the light was too dim for sewing, outsinging the calls of our parents. We sang loudly at first, each voice outstriding the other. Shortly, an esthetic emerged; sad parts were sung heartbreakingly softly, jolly parts were sung jauntily but never coarsely shouted. We became divas, operatic actresses like Geraldine Farrar and Rosa Raisa, capable of melting the cement sidewalk with "Because I love you, I've tried so hard but can't forget," with "Not for just an hour, not for just a day, not for just a year, But Always."

BROOKLYN HEIGHTS

1.

I'm on Water Street in Brooklyn,
between the Brooklyn Bridge
and the Manhattan Bridge,
the high charge of their traffic
filling the empty street.
Abandoned warehouses
on either side.
In the shadowed doorways, shades
of Melville and Murder Incorporated.
Five o'clock October light.
Jets and gulls in the fleecy sky.
Climbing the hill to Columbia Heights,
I turn to see the cordage
of the Brooklyn Bridge, and behind it
the battle-gray Manhattan.

2.

This room shelved high with books
echoes with my midnights. Pages
of useless lines swim in it. Only
now and then a voice cuts through
saying something right: No sound
is dissonant which tells of life.
The gaudy ensigns of this life
flash in the streets; a December light,
whipped by wind, is at the windows.
Even now the English poets are in the street,
Keats and Coleridge on Hicks Street,
heading for the Bridge. Swayed aloft there,
the lower bay before them, they can
bring me back my City line by line.

Harvey Shapiro
from *The Light Holds*
1984

PETER SIS

HARVEY DINNERSTEIN

Edmund Wilson

Memoirs of Hecate County

1942

...so I decided to go over to Brooklyn and find out what the situation was.

I had never seen her house or her family, and the journey brought a certain suspense. When I went down into the black dugout of the subway and took the train that banged and hurtled through the straight narrow tube, it was as if I were engaging myself in some logical course of procedure which would force me to a harsh recognition I had hitherto kept at a distance. We shot out of the tunnel at Brooklyn Bridge, and I looked down, through the rows of dark girders that wove back and forth like a mechanical loom, on the city shown in dark silhouette above a livid and leaden water that seemed to shine at one edge white-hot, and on those streets of the East Side, where Anna had been born, with their roofs packed tight and dingy for miles, shouting here at the escaping trains, from the walls and the tops of their buildings, their last cries to come and buy fine values—in raincoats, in furs, in candy, in laxatives, in five-cent cigars; and I was caught for a moment by a vision of that immensity of anonymous life, which, though I knew it only through Anna, had thus far come for me alive at one point like the screen in the blotted theatre that is peopled by the animated shadows of persons not really present, whom one may never see in the flesh—though in this case I knew that they existed and had the heat and the accents of life and that the dramas they acted were real; and I was moved by a kind of awe. Then we went down into the blackness again, and finally emerged from the tunnel in a raw landscape of tracks and garages, gas tanks, one-story factories and bleak little cheap brick houses in which the factory workers evidently lived. This was Anna's own country, I said to myself; I might as well accept it at once.

But I was surprised when I got out at the stop which was closest to Anna's address. I walked along under low-columned cloisters, pale brown and a little more gracious than anything connected with the subway on the Manhattan side of the bridge; and emerged from the subway steps into the sunlight of a whole new world, which seemed to me inexplicably attractive. It was Twelfth Street just off King's Highway, not far from Coney Island and Brighton Beach; and there was space and ocean air and light, and what seemed to me—it was what most astonished me—an atmosphere of freedom and leisure quite unknown on the other side. The great thing here was that there were so few high buildings—the tallest were apartment houses that ran only to six or eight stories, and there were not very many of these; and for the rest, one found little brick shops—delicatessen stores, beauty parlors, drugstores, billiard rooms, kosher butchers, and newsstands with Italian and Jewish papers—that had been relatively newly built and that looked absolutely toylike. These cropped up in patches at intervals among streets that were exceptionally wide and that seemed to go on forever, yet, more or less of a sameness though they were, had somehow escaped from the abstract monotony characteristic of American cities. They were planted with rows of young maples, now beginning to be green with April; and the houses—double affairs though they were—placed each at a

HENRIK DRESCHER

good distance from its neighbors, seemed quite independent dwellings, not unpleasantly paired, rather than cramping partitioned units, and though they were all fairly small, had been planned with rather an amiable eye to the amenities—for each had its own little backyard and garage and its little privet hedge on the street, its latticed shades in the windows, its arched doorway with a diadem of bricks that rayed out around the top, and its little flight of steps in front with an ornamental patterned stone bowl in which nasturtiums or geraniums grew. These avenues and houses were further redeemed from their tendency toward uniformity by the children with whom they were populated and who, even in this period of poverty, seemed remarkably healthy and clean. There were babies being wheeled in baby-carriages that had what seemed to be a great luxury of springs and young girls with mature round breasts that bulged out under the surfaces of their sweaters; and there were also their ample mothers leaning out of the ground-floor front windows, and occasionally a black-browed Sicilian in suburban American clothes tinkering with his car, or an old Jew walking solemnly and stiffly, a derby hat on the front of his head, pulled down over his somber eyes.

F. Scott Fitzgerald

My Lost City

1932

It was three years before we saw New York again. As the ship glided up the river, the city burst thunderously upon us in the early dusk—the white glacier of lower New York swooping down like a strand of a bridge to rise into uptown New York, a miracle of foamy light suspended by the stars. A band started to play on deck, but the majesty of the city made the march trivial and tinkling. From that moment I knew that New York, however often I might leave it, was home.

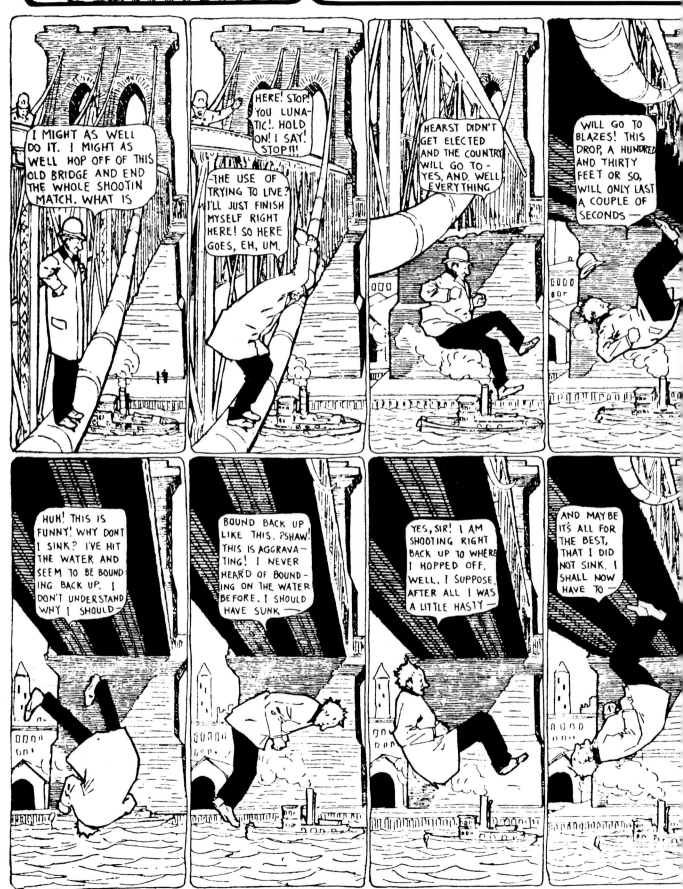

WINSOR McCAY

Thomas Wolfe
Enchanted City
from *The Web and the Rock*
1939

For the city has a million faces, and just as it is said that no two men can really know what each is thinking of, what either sees when he speaks of "red" or "blue," so can no man ever know just what another means when he tells about the city that he sees. For the city that he sees is just the city that he brings with him, that he has within his heart and even at that immeasurable moment of first perception, when for the first time he sees the city with his naked eye, at that tremendous moment of final apprehension when the great city smites at last upon his living sense, still no man can be certain he has seen the city as it is, because in the hairbreadth of that instant recognition a whole new city is composed, made out of sense but shaped and colored and unalterable from all that he has felt and thought and dreamed about before.

Robert Benchley
The Benchley Roundup
1928

For most visitors to Manhattan, both foreign and domestic, New York is the Shrine of the Good Time. This is only natural, for outsiders come to New York for the sole purpose of having a good time, and it is for their New York hosts to provide it. The visiting Englishman, or the visiting Californian, is convinced that New York City is made up of millions of gay pixies, flitting about constantly in a sophisticated manner in search of a new thrill. "I don't see how you stand it," they often say to the native New Yorker who has been sitting up past his bedtime for a week in an attempt to tire his guest out. "It's all right for a week or so, but give me the little old home town when it comes to *living.*" And, under his breath, the New Yorker endorses the transfer and wonders himself how he stands it.

The New York pixie element is seen by visitors because the visitors go where the pixie element is to be found, having become, for the nonce, pixies themselves. If they happen to be authors in search of copy, they perhaps go slumming to those places where they have heard the Other Half lives. They don't want to be narrow about the thing. There are the East Side pushcarts, which they must see and write a chapter about under the title of "The Melting Pot." Greenwich Village they have heard about, but that only fortifies their main thesis that New York is a gay, irresponsible nest of hedonists. Wall Street comes next, with its turmoil and tall buildings—rush-rush-rush-money-money-money! These ingredients, together with material gathered at the Coffee House Club and private dinners, and perhaps a short summary of the gang situation, all go into a word picture called "New York," and the author sails for home, giving out an interview at the pier in which he says that the city is pleasure-mad and its women are cold and beautiful.

Typical of the method by which the actualities of New York are

taken by writers and translated into material for the New York of their dreams is the fantasy indulged in by Mr. Ford (in common, it must be admitted, with most of our domestic writers) of attributing the lights in the buildings along lower Manhattan to some province of fairyland.

"By day the soaring cliffs," writes Mr. Ford, "that rise joyously over behind the Battery are symbols not merely of hope but of attainment; after dark, and more particularly in the dusk, they are sheer fairyland. There is something particularly romantic in a Germanic sort of way about mountains illuminated from within... the million-wise illumination of New York is a lighter, gayer affair... the mind on seeing it connotes not subterranean picks and sweat but lighter more tenuous occupations—the pursuits of delicate, wayward beings."

Our visitors are confronted with so much gaiety in New York, especially where the lights are brightest, that they fall into the literary error of ascribing any metropolitan utilization of voltage to the pursuit of pleasure. And it *is* difficult to look at the lighted windows at the end of the island and not idealize them into some sort of manifestation of joy and exuberance. But if the writers who thrill so at the sight and translate it into terms of New York's lightheartedness could, by some sardonic and unkind force, be projected along any one of those million beams of fairy light, they would find that it came directly from an office peopled by tired Middle Westerners, New Englanders, and Southerners, each

SEYMOUR CHWAST

watching the clock as lighting-up time comes, not to start out on a round of merrymaking but to embark on a long subway ride uptown. And this ride will take them on past the haunts that the visitors and their hosts know, past the clubs and theatres and squash courts, to an enormous city above One Hundred and Twenty-fifth Street, where life is, with the exception of a certain congestion in living quarters, exactly the same as life in Muncie, Indiana, or Quincy, Illinois. For the inhabitants of this city have come direct from Muncie and Quincy and have never become assimilated into the New York of the commentators. It is not even picturesque, as the East Side is picturesque. It is a melting pot where the ingredients refuse to melt. The people are just as much New Yorkers as those in the Forties, and they outnumber the "typical" New Yorkers to so great an extent that an intramural battle between the two elements could not possibly last for more than twenty minutes, even if the pixies had machine guns.

EPITAPH FOR ANY NEW YORKER

I, who all my life had hurried,
    Came to Peter's crowded gate;
And, as usual, was worried,
    Fearing that I might be late.
So, when I began to jostle
    (I forgot that I was dead)
Patient smiled the old Apostle:
    "Take your Eternity," he said.

Christopher Morley
1923

Floyd Dell

Love in Greenwich Village

1926

It was, for all of us, a life that was quaintly enriched by our poverty. How otherwise, except by being very poor, should we ever have learned to make the most of those joys that are so cheap, or that cost nothing at all, the joys of comradeship and play and mere childlike fun? When someone had sold something, we trailed across Washington Square to spend the money gorgeously in the basement of the Brevoort; but when there was no such luck, there was always the Staten Island ferry, or the Fifth Avenue bus—and always and always there was talk to keep us up till dawn. I remember an evening of still more infantile folly, when Theodore Dreiser and a table full of painters and poets and actresses and editors played "Up Jenkins!"—a noisy, rowdy, childish game with much thumping on the table and shouting and laughter—in one of those basement restaurants, forgetful of time, until we were interrupted by a policeman who had been drawn from blocks away by the sounds of our abandoned revelry—and we realized that it was nearly dawn, and that we had been alone in the place for hours! The next time I see Dreiser, I will remind him of that incident; he will grin sheepishly, and unfold and refold his handkerchief, and rock back and forth in his perpetual rocking-chair, and say: "A mad world, my masters!"

Will Rogers
New York's Five Boroughs Celebrate
1923

New York is in the midst of what they call a Silver Jubilee. It's celebrating the 25th anniversary of something, nobody can find out just what. There is no reason to just pick out 25 years and start celebrating it. But I think the reason was that this was as far back as any of them connected with the city could remember. Personally, I think it was to celebrate the starting of the Hat Checking privilege, which originated here and was successfully copied everywhere else, but never with the finesse that it has in the mother lodge here.

Or, on account of being called a Silver Jubilee, it may be celebrating the passing away of all silver coins, as that small denomination vanished entirely here.

They have an exhibit representing progress, showing how much faster we can cross the streets compared to what we used to. Now it's a run, and if you don't make it, and the probabilities are you won't, they show how quick they can get you to the hospital, so you can die there instead of en route, as you used to.

Then they show the modern hearses, which go so fast they have killed more people than they carried. You know, we don't stop to realize it now; but in the old days it was nothing for a man to be late to his own funeral. But now, if you are going to a friend's funeral and happen to be held up in a traffic jam a few minutes, you will arrive there just as his widow is coming out of the church with the next husband, counting the insurance money.

Also, in this exhibition of progress of 25 years, they show the old saloons where you had to walk to the corner to even get a drink. With the modern method it's brought right to your home.

It showed how the city's money was spent for city government. Not all of it, of course, but the 20 per cent which is spent for it, it showed.

It showed police methods years ago compared to now. In the old days they had to hunt till they found the crook. With modern methods they have his fingerprints, so what's the use getting him, if you know who he is. Then, if he ever surrenders, you know if he's telling the truth, or not.

It also showed the art of ticket speculating and its advancement. An Irishman named Louie was the only one in town 25 years ago; now there are hundreds of them in offices where a stranger in the city can go and buy tickets for the last row, without going near the box office.

It showed that 25 years ago they still had a few street cars pulled by horses, but they were up on street level, and were very unsanitary—bad air and everything. Now it shows you how you can be in a nice tunnel under the ground where the air is good. You know it is good because there have been hundreds using it before you got a hold of it.

Then, if you got stuck in old cars, you had to walk to get another car. But now, you can stay right under there, sometimes all day, and read over somebody's shoulder and not get out at all. Oh, I tell you, things do move.

Of course they had a parade. Everything nowadays has to annoy with a parade. They gave all the city employees a day off without pay, and all they had to do was to march 20 miles.

Christopher Morley
Skyline
from *New York World's Fair 1939 Prospectus*
1936

Under what star was granted me
To live immersed where I can see
Her terrible tall majesty?
Who fated it
That I should squander youth and wit
To see her blaze and ride so high
On peacock sky?

Wind of what hazard came to sow
My mortal dust where I could know
Her comedy, both high and low,
Her evenings lit
With pride and lustre infinite;
Servant of all her changing moods
And magnitudes.

Town of all towns earth ever knew,
Sierra-man made on the blue
Miraculous to thought and view,
I only ask
To make your madrigal my task
Where rhyming perpendiculars
Reach toward the stars.

Sorceress beyond compare,
City of glory and despair
So terraced on the Western air,
Your music pour
Over and round me evermore,
Symphony fatal and divine
City of mine.

Hall of Marine Transportation, New York World's Fair 1939

The Ford Motor Company Building, New York World's Fair 1939

The General Motors Building, New York World's Fair 1939

Court of Peace, New York World's Fair 1939

The Aviation Building, New York World's Fair 1939

The Du Pont Building, New York World's Fair 1939

General Electric Building, New York World's Fair 1939

The United States Steel Building, New York World's Fair 1939

Statue of Liberty
at Night
New York City

Sinclair Lewis

That Was New York and That Was Me

1937

London, Paris, Berlin, Rome, Vienna, San Francisco—I have found them to be comfortable and easily familiar cities. If no cit talks to you in London, the bobbies do give you directions. If in Paris on a wet day the taxis skid three times to the block, no one is ever hurt save in the vocabulary. But New York is still to me very much what it was on that September evening in 1903. O. O. McIntyre can have it. As for me, I would not take taxi from, say, Ninetieth Street to the Village even to go to a party at which the presence was guaranteed, under penalty, of Gandhi, Stephen S. Wise, Dr. Harvey Cushing, General Göring, Bernarr Macfadden, Evangeline Booth, and J. Edgar Hoover complete with sawed-off shotgun. My first day in New York has never quite ended. And eighty cents still seems too much to pay for orange juice.

Theodore Dreiser

My City

1929

Nowhere is there anything like it. My City. Not London. Not Paris. Not Moscow. Not any city I have ever seen. So strong. So immense. So elate.

Its lilt! Its power to hurry the blood in one's veins, to make one sing, to weep, to make one hate or sigh and die. Yet in the face of defeat, loneliness, despair, the dragging of feet in sheer weariness, perhaps, what strong, good days! Winey, electric! What beauty! What impressiveness! Neither hungry days nor yet lonely nor hopeless ones have ever broken this impressiveness—this spell for me.

A cruel and brutal city by turns; a callous, money-seeking and unsentimental city, as one looks here and there. But lyric, too. And spendthrift. Frittering, idle, wasteful—saving nothing, hoarding nothing, unless maybe, unmarketable dreams. And dreaming so, even in the face of brutality and calculation. Yet, in the face of this strain, failure, none of its lyric days going unnoted, none of its spell evaded. They have burst on me—its days—with shouts, with song, a sense of deathless verse—or have come crawling, weeping, opening and closing in despair. Yet to this hour I cannot step out of my door save with a thrill responsive to it all— its grandeur, mystery, glory—yea, Babylonian eternity....

It is as old and as young as I am. As curious and as indifferent. Amid all the stupendous wealth of it a man may die of hunger—a minute atom of a man or child, and so easily fed. And where there is so much wherewith to feed. Or of loneliness—where millions are lonely and seeking heartease, the pressure of a single friendly hand. Ho! one may cry aloud for aid and not be heard; ask for words only and harvest silence only, where yet all is blare. Or be harried by too much contact, and fail of peace; be driven, harried, buried by attention. God!

And yet for all its this or that, here it runs, like a great river; beats and thunders like a tumultuous sea; or yawns or groans or shrieks or howls in sheer ennui.

I never step out but I note it. Yet I never step out but I think, ha! power, energy, strength, life, beauty, terror! And the astounding mystery of it all! You—I—all of us—with our eager, futile dreams. We are here together, seeking much, straining much. You, I. We are yearning to do so much here in my city—be so much—have some one group or phase or audience, or mayhap one other somewhere in all this, to recognize just us—just you—me. And not always finding that one. My fateful city!

Mark Twain

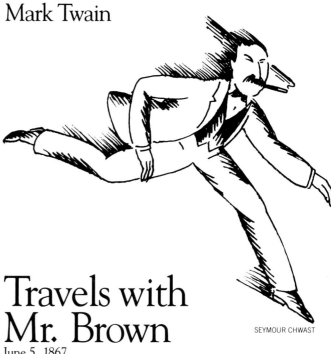

SEYMOUR CHWAST

Travels with Mr. Brown

June 5, 1867

...I have at last, after several months' experience, made up my mind that it [New York] is a splendid desert—a domed and steepled solitude, where a stranger is lonely in the midst of a million of his race. A man walks his tedious miles through the same interminable street every day, elbowing his way through a buzzing multitude of men, yet never seeing a familiar face, and never seeing a strange one the second time.... Every man seems to feel that he has got the duties of two lifetimes to accomplish in one, and so he rushes, rushes, rushes, and never has time to be companionable —never has any time at his disposal to fool away on matters which do not involve dollars and duty and business.

All this has a tendency to make the city-bred man impatient of interruption, suspicious of strangers, and fearful of being bored, and his business interfered with. The natural result is...the serene indifference of the New Yorker to everybody and everything without the pale of his private and individual circle.

There is something in this ceaseless buzz, and hurry, and bustle, that keeps a stranger in a state of unwholesome excitement all the time, and makes him restless and uneasy...a something which impels him to try to do everything, and yet permits him to do nothing....A stranger feels unsatisfied, here, a good part of the time. He starts to a library; changes, and moves toward a theatre; changes again and thinks he will visit a friend; goes within a biscuit-toss of a picture-gallery, a billiard-room, a beer-cellar and a circus, in succession, and finally drifts home and to bed, without having really done anything or gone anywhere.

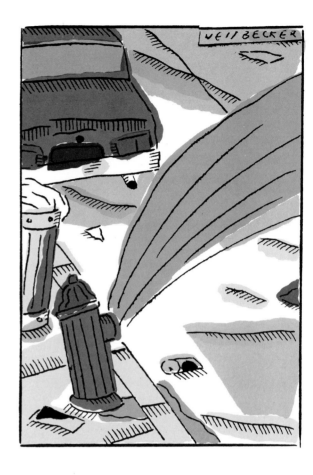

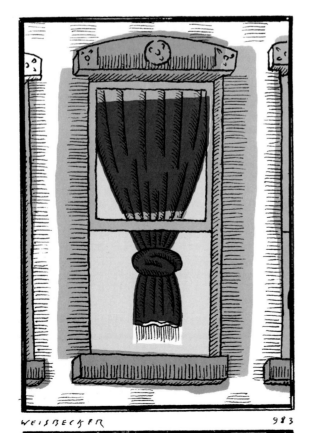

PHILIPPE WEISBECKER

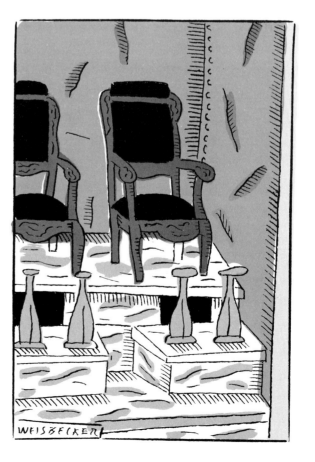

SEYMOUR CHWAST

Weegee
Sunday Morning in Manhattan
1945

This is the most peaceful time of the whole week. Everything is so quiet...no traffic noises...and no crime either. People are just too exhausted for anything. The Sunday papers, all bundled up, are thrown on the sidewalk in front of the still-closed candy stores and newspaper stands. New Yorkers like their Sunday papers, especially the lonely men and women who live in furnished rooms. They leave early to get the papers...they get two. One of the standard-size papers, either the *Times* or *Tribune*...they're thick and heavy, plenty of reading in them, and then also the tabloid *Mirror*...to read Winchell and learn all about Cafe Society and the Broadway playboys and their Glamour Girl Friends. Then back to the room...to read and read...to drive away loneliness...but one tires of reading. One wants someone to talk to, to argue with, and yes, someone to make love to. How about a movie—NO—too damn much talking on the screen. "But Darling I do love you...RAHLLY I do,"...then the final clinch with the lovers in each other's arms...then it's even worse, to go back alone to the furnished room...to look up at the ceiling and cry oneself to sleep.

Edward Field
New York
1977

I live in a beautiful place, a city
people claim to be astonished
when you say you live there.
They talk of junkies, muggings, dirt, and noise,
missing the point completely.

I tell them where they live it is hell,
a land of frozen people.
They never think of people.

Home, I am astonished by this environment
that is also a form of nature
like those paradises of trees and grass

but this is a people paradise
where we are the creatures mostly
though thank God for dogs, cats, sparrows, and roaches.

This vertical place is no more an accident
than the Himalayas are.
The city needs all those tall buildings
to contain the tremendous energy here.
The landscape is in a state of balance.
We do God's will whether we know it or not:
Where I live the streets end in a river of sunlight.

Nowhere else in the country do people
show just what they feel—
we don't put on any act.
Look at the way New Yorkers
walk down the street. It says,
I don't care. What nerve,
to dare to live their dreams, or nightmares,
and no one bothers to look.

True, you have to be an expert to live here.
Part of the trick is not to go anywhere, lounge about,
go slowly in the midst of the rush for novelty.
Anyway, beside the eats the big event here
is the streets which are full of love—
we hug and kiss a lot. You can't say that
for anywhere else around. For some
it is the sex part they care about and get—
there's all the opportunity in the world if you want it.
For me it is different:
Out walking, my soul seeks its food.
It knows what it wants.
Instantly it recognizes its mate, our eyes meet,
and our beings exchange a vital energy,
the universe goes on Charge
and we pass by without holding.

TONY SARG

John Updike
Central Park
1956

On the afternoon of the first day of spring, when the gutters were still heaped high with Monday's snow but the sky itself was swept clean, we put on our galoshes and walked up the sunny side of Fifth Avenue to Central Park. There we saw:

Great black rocks emerging from the melting drifts, their craggy skins glistening like the backs of resurrected brontosaurs.

A pigeon on the half-frozen pond strutting to the edge of the ice and looking a duck in the face.

A policeman getting his shoe wet testing the ice.

Three elderly relatives trying to coax a little boy to accompany his father on a sled ride down a short but steep slope. After much balking, the boy did, and, sure enough, the sled tipped over and the father got his collar full of snow. Everybody laughed except the boy, who sniffled.

Four boys in black leather jackets throwing snowballs at each other. (The snow was ideally soggy, and packed hard with one squeeze.)

Seven men without hats.

Twelve snowmen, none of them intact.

Two men listening to the radio in a car parked outside the Zoo; Mel Allen was broadcasting the Yanks–Cardinals game from St. Petersburg.

A tahr (*Hemitragus jemlaicus*) pleasantly squinting in the sunlight.

An aoudad absently pawing the mud and chewing.

A yak with its back turned.

Empty cages labelled "Coati," "Orang-outang," "Ocelot."

A father saying to his little boy, who was annoyed almost to tears by the inactivity of the seals, "Father [Father Seal, we as-

sumed] is very tired; he worked hard all day."

Most of the cafeteria's out-of-doors tables occupied.

A pretty girl in black pants falling on them at the Wollman Memorial Rink.

"BILL & DORIS" carved on a tree. "REX & RITA" written in the snow.

Two old men playing, and six supervising, a checkers game.

The Michael Friedsam Foundation Merry-Go-Round, nearly empty of children but overflowing with calliope music.

A man on a bench near the carrousel reading, through sunglasses, a book on economics.

Crews of shinglers repairing the roof of the Tavern-on-the-Green.

A woman dropping a camera she was trying to load, the film unrolling in the slush and exposing itself.

A little colored boy in aviator goggles rubbing his ears and saying, "He really hurt me." "No, he didn't," his nursemaid told him.

The green head of Giuseppe Mazzini staring across the white softball field, unblinking, though the sun was in its eyes.

Water murmuring down walks and rocks and steps. A grown man trying to block one rivulet with snow.

Things like brown sticks nosing through a plot of cleared soil.

A tire track in a piece of mud far removed from where any automobiles could be.

Footprints around a KEEP OFF sign.

Two pigeons feeding each other.

Two showgirls, whose faces had not yet thawed the frost of their makeup, treading indignantly through the slush.

A plump old man saying "Chick, chick" and feeding peanuts to squirrels.

Many solitary men throwing snowballs at tree trunks.

Many birds calling to each other about how little the Ramble has changed.

One red mitten lying lost under a poplar tree.

An airplane, very bright and distant, slowly moving through the branches of a sycamore.

Pete Hamill
The Invisible City
1980

Usually in the fall of the year Sullivan loved the smell of burning leaves. But today, sitting in the yard of his house in Lynbrook, he felt a dull unease, a fugitive sense of the end of things and the arrival of a last season. He sat in the folding aluminum chair drinking a whiskey and soda, with the newspapers on the ground beside him. Leaves were scattered across his yard but he had not yet gathered them; the rake leaned against the white fence, a challenge to act. He didn't move.

He heard sounds inside the house. His wife was back from Mass, and he heard a dish clack against a table and imagined her sliding the roast into the oven and checking the ice and the cake and all the other things they would need for the party. It was his birthday and the children and their wives and their children were all coming, but he had no sense of approaching feast or celebration. He could retire now, under the new plan the company had put together; he could pick up the retirement pay and the pension, someone would give him a gold watch at a Chinese restaurant and he could come out here and burn leaves and sit quietly and, in baseball season, watch all the day games. Forty-six years of work were over, if he wanted them to be over.

"Another drink, Michael?" his wife asked, appearing suddenly in the doorway.

"Sure," he said, without looking around: seeing in his mind's eye her worn, handsome face, thinking that the Irishwoman's face improves as it ages, that this surely must have something to do with acceptance. She took his glass but he stared ahead, watching the smoke drift away into the clear sky. He suddenly remembered her when she was sixteen and they lived four blocks away from each other on Fourth Avenue in Brooklyn; she had lustrous brown hair then and a smile that broke hearts, and for some reason he remembered proposing to her on a bench in Sunset Park and how they had walked home together in the hot night with their lives spread out before them.

That was the year Babe Ruth hit the sixty home runs, and part of him always turned on the TV set hoping to see the Babe's spindly legs and hulking body and the lovely swing and the ball sailing away to the sky. Gene Tunney was the heavyweight champion and Jimmy Walker was the mayor of New York, and he remembered how everyone that year had tried to dress like the mayor, with narrow suits and snap-brim hats, and how they really looked like Legs Diamond.

"They should be here soon," his wife said, handing him the drink.

"Kitty, what was the name of that speakeasy we used to go to on Seventh Avenue?"

She laughed in a surprised, almost girlish way.

"The speakeasy on Seventh Avenue? Oh, Michael, I don't remember..."

The telephone rang and she turned and went back into the house. Flanagan's, Sullivan thought: something like that. Irish. Flanagan's or Harrigan's.

He remembered now the trolley car with slats on the floor that rattled across the Brooklyn Bridge, and the way a snowstorm looked as it moved across the harbor, with the Statue of Liberty lost in the gray swirl, and tugs shoving barges up the East River. It had been his own secret journey: made alone in the mornings and the evenings. And he remembered the private sense of the city's emptiness that came late at night down in Wall Street when he worked late, and the lights burning in the old *World* building on Park Row. He remembered going around Broadway with the others after a big fight, and he wondered if anyone remembered how Jimmy McLarnin threw the hook and what had happened to all of the people he had known in those years before the war.

"That was Jimmy," his wife said. "He'll be late."

Jimmy, he thought, was always late. He had named him after Jimmy Walker, and he remembered how the boy looked when he was ten—blond hair and square shoulders—and the day they had followed the moving truck all the way out to Lynbrook in 1946, with Jackie sitting in the back, Kitty between him and Tommy, Jimmy beside him, and how he had known that day that New York was forever behind him.

They had gone to Lynbrook for the children: he remembered the conversations over the kitchen table in the old neighborhood, the careful calculations about the money, the talk about how the kids needed fresh air and good schools. And now Jackie was already working on his second marriage; Jimmy had worked at fifteen jobs in ten years; Tommy was a drunk.

They were his children and he somehow loved them, but he watched the smoke in the backyards and wondered why he remembered everything that happened before the war and nothing much that happened after; he remembered New York and the rest was a blur; he remembered Jimmy Walker but he couldn't remember who was mayor before Wagner.

He heard a car pull into the driveway, making a grating sound on the pebbles, and then a car door slamming.

"It was Rattigan's," he said triumphantly. "It was Patty Rattigan's!"

He turned and his son Jackie was standing there alone, looking puzzled.

"What was Rattigan's?" Jackie asked.

Sullivan looked away, watching the smoke. "Oh, just a place I was trying to remember," he said. "Nothing important."

He stood, his son embraced him briskly and he started into the house to see his grandchildren, thinking of snow falling on the streets of New York and the luster of a girl's brown hair.

LOU BEACH

Gregory Corso
New York, True North
1964

I don't feel it like a Broadway musical—none of this "New York, New York, it's a wonderful town"—but the city really makes me look at the people and see that they're almost a community. You go to a barbershop, they don't talk *low,* and everybody understands everything. I went in for a shave. The man said, "You need a haircut." I said, "I don't *think* I need one." "Well," he told me, "if you don't need a haircut, you don't need a shave, either," and everyone in the shop heard this and they all broke up laughing. I broke up too. I said, "Great." Everyone's on the ball in their consciousness, you see, and New York really is not square at all. In other words, you can be real crazy and not be thought of as merely an eccentric. Everybody is kind of batty in a way, anyway.

Whenever I met anybody in Europe who was very intelligent, and if they hadn't been to New York, I would feel something lacking in their intelligence. Then I got back and met some people here who have been putting New York down. I said, "What you have to do to appreciate the city is go out of it." Coming back on the boat was great—six in the morning, the sun was breaking through. Everybody rushed to look at the Statue of Liberty on the left-hand side. I stayed on the right-hand side and gazed at the parachute jump at Coney Island, and I said, "Ah, America's Eiffel Tower." And looked at the old Half Moon Hotel, it used to be, and I said, "Ah, Abie Reles." New York is a good place for a poet, because it is high class and a poet is high class. It's wonderful to be born a poet in the greatest country in the world, and to be born a poet in the greatest city in the greatest country in the world is the greatest blessing.

ANDREZJ CZECOT

Allen Ginsberg
Waking in New York

1968

PART II

On the roof cloudy sky fading sun rays
            electric torches atop—
         auto horns—The towers
   with time-hands giant pointing
            late Dusk hour over
                  clanky roofs

Tenement streets' brick sagging cornices
         baby white kite fluttering against giant
            insect face-gill Electric Mill
               smokestacked blue & fumes drift up
      Red messages, shining high floors,
         Empire State dotted with tiny windows
            lit, across the blocks
      of spire, steeple, golden topped utility
            building roofs—far like
               pyramids lit in jagged
                  desert rocks—

The giant the giant city awake
         in the first warm breath of springtime
Waking voices, babble of Spanish
         street families, radio music
            floating under roofs, longhaired
               announcer sincerity squawking
                     cigar voice
         Light zips up phallos stories
            beneath red antennae needling
               thru rooftop chimnies' smog
                  black drift thru the blue air—
Bridges curtained by uplit apartment walls,
         one small tower with a light
            on its shoulder below the "moody, water-loving
                        giants"

The giant stacks burn thick grey
         smoke, Chrysler is lit with green,
down Wall street islands of skyscraper
         black jagged in Sabbath quietness—
Oh fathers, how I am alone in this
            vast human wilderness
Houses uplifted like hives off
         the stone floor of the world—
   the city too vast to know, too
            myriad windowed to govern
               from ancient halls—

"O edifice of gas!"—Sun shafts
         descend on the highest building's
            striped blocktop a red light
               winks buses hiss & rush
            grinding, green lights
            of north bridges,
                  hum roar & Tarzan
                     squeal, whistle
                        swoops, hurrahs!

Is someone dying in all this stone building?
Child poking its black head out of the womb
            like the pupil of an eye?
Am I not breathing here frightened
                  and amazed—?
Where is my comfort, where's heart-ease,
         Where are tears of joy?
Where are the companions? in
         deep homes in Stuyvesant Town.
         behind the yellow-window wall?
I fail, book fails,—a lassitude,
            a fear—tho I'm alive
and gaze over the descending—No!
peek in the inky beauty of the roofs.

E. B. White
Here Is New York

1949

A poem compresses much in a small space and adds music, thus heightening its meaning. The city is like poetry: it compresses all life, all races and breeds, into a small island and adds music and the accompaniment of internal engines. The island of Manhattan is without any doubt the greatest human concentrate on earth, the poem whose magic is comprehensible to millions of permanent residents but whose full meaning will always remain illusive. At the feet of the tallest and plushiest offices lie the crummiest slums. The genteel mysteries housed in the Riverside Church are only a few blocks from the voodoo charms of Harlem. The merchant princes, riding to Wall Street in their limousines down the East River Drive, pass within a few hundred yards of the gypsy kings; but the princes do not know they are passing kings, and the kings are not up yet anyway—they live a more leisurely life than the princes and get drunk more consistently.

New York is nothing like Paris; it is nothing like London; and it is not Spokane multiplied by sixty, or Detroit multiplied by four. It is by all odds the loftiest of cities. It even managed to reach the highest point in the sky at the lowest moment of the depression. The Empire State Building shot twelve hundred and fifty feet into the air when it was madness to put out as much as six inches of new growth. (The building has a mooring mast that no dirigible has ever tied to; it employs a man to flush toilets in slack times; it has been hit by an airplane in a fog, struck countless times by lightning, and been jumped off of by so many unhappy people that pedestrians instinctively quicken step when passing Fifth Avenue and 34th Street.)

Manhattan has been compelled to expand skyward because of the absence of any other direction in which to grow. This, more than any other thing, is responsible for its physical majesty. It is to the nation what the white church spire is to the village—the visible symbol of aspiration and faith, the white plume saying that the way is up. The summer traveler swings in over Hell Gate Bridge and from the window of his sleeping car as it glides above the pigeon lofts and back yards of Queens looks southwest to where the morning light first strikes the steel peaks of midtown, and he sees its upward thrust unmistakable: the great walls and towers rising, the smoke rising, the heat not yet rising, the hopes and ferments of so many awakening millions rising—this vigorous spear that presses heaven hard.

STEFAN MROZEWSKI

John Steinbeck
The Making of a New Yorker
1953

New York is the only city I have ever lived in. I have lived in the country, in the small town, and in New York. It is true I have had apartments in San Francisco, Mexico City, Los Angeles, Paris, and sometimes have stayed for months, but that is a very different thing. As far as homes go, there is only a small California town and New York. This is a matter of feeling.

The transition from small town to New York is a slow and rough process. I am writing it not because I think my experience was unique; quite the contrary. I suspect that the millions of New Yorkers who were not born here have had much the same experience—at least parallel experiences....

When I came the first time to New York in 1925 I had never been to a city in my life. I arrived on a boat, tourist, one hundred dollars. It was November....

From a porthole, then, I saw the city, and it horrified me. There was something monstrous about it—the tall buildings looming to the sky and the lights shining through the falling snow. I crept ashore—frightened and cold and with a touch of panic in my stomach. This Dick Whittington didn't even have a cat.

I wasn't really bad off. I had a sister in New York and she had a good job. She had a husband and he had a good job. My brother-in-law got me a job as a laborer and I found a room three flights up in Fort Greene Place in Brooklyn. That is about as alone as you can get....

I was going to live in New York but I was going to avoid it. I planted a lawn in the garden, bought huge pots and planted tomatoes, pollinating the blossoms with a water-color brush. But I can see now that a conspiracy was going on, of which I was not even aware. I walked miles through the streets for the exercise, and began to know the butcher and the newsdealer and the liquor man, not as props or as enemies but as people.

I have talked to many people about this and it seems to be a kind of mystical experience. The preparation is unconscious, the realization happens in a flaming second. It was on Third Avenue. The trains were grinding over my head. The snow was nearly waist-high in the gutters and uncollected garbage was scattered in the dirty mess. The wind was cold, and frozen pieces of paper went scraping along the pavement. I stopped to look in a drug-store window where a latex cooch dancer was undulated by a concealed motor—and something burst in my head, a kind of light and a kind of feeling blended into an emotion which if it had spoken would have said, "My God! I belong here. Isn't this wonderful?"

Everything fell into place. I saw every face I passed. I noticed every doorway and the stairways to apartments. I looked across the street at the windows, lace curtains and potted geraniums through sooty glass. It was beautiful—but most important, I was part of it. I was no longer a stranger. I had become a New Yorker.

*   *   *

Now there may be people who move easily into New York without travail, but most I have talked to about it have had some kind of trial by torture before acceptance. And the acceptance is a double thing. It seems to me that the city finally accepts you just as you finally accept the city.

Joseph Mitchell
The Bottom of the Harbor
1959

Every now and then, seeking to rid my mind of thoughts of death and doom, I get up early and go down to Fulton Fish Market. I usually arrive around five-thirty, and take a walk through the two huge open-fronted market sheds, the Old Market and the New Market, whose fronts rest on South Street and whose backs rest on piles in the East River. At that time, a little while before the trading begins, the stands in the sheds are heaped high and spilling over with forty to sixty kinds of finfish and shellfish from the East Coast, the West Coast, the Gulf Coast, and half a dozen foreign countries. The smoky riverbank dawn, the racket the fishmongers make, the seaweedy smell, and the sight of this plentifulness always give me a feeling of well-being, and sometimes they elate me. I wander among the stands for an hour or so. Then I go into a cheerful market restaurant named Sloppy Louie's and eat a big, inexpensive, invigorating breakfast—a kippered herring and scrambled eggs, or a shad-roe omelet, or split sea scallops and bacon, or some other breakfast specialty of the place.

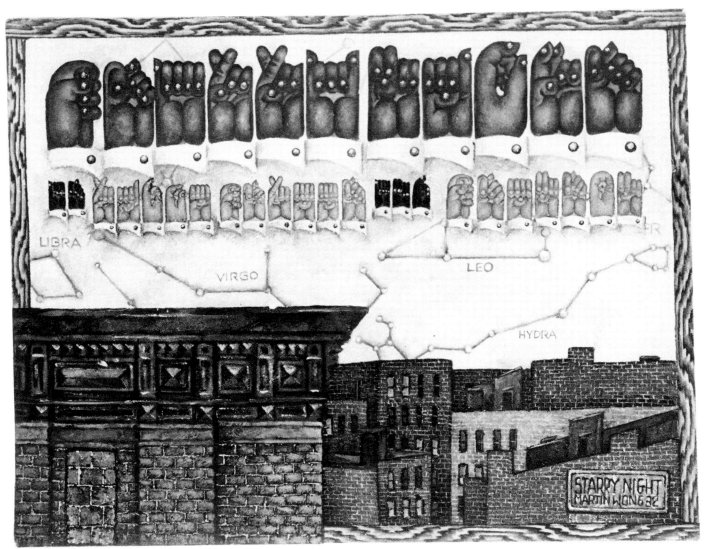

MARTIN WONG

A young man in a small town, a frog in a small puddle, if he kicks his feet is able to make waves, get mud in his neighbor's eyes—make some impression. He is known. His family is known. People watch him with some interest, whether kindly or maliciously. He comes to New York and no matter what he does, no one is impressed. He challenges the city to fight and it licks him without being aware of him. This is a dreadful blow to a small-town ego. He hates the organism that ignores him. He hates the people who look through him.

And then one day he falls into place, accepts the city and does not fight it any more. It is too huge to notice him and suddenly the fact that it doesn't notice him becomes the most delightful thing in the world. His self-consciousness evaporates. If he is dressed superbly well—there are half a million people dressed equally well. If he is in rags—there are a million ragged people. If he is tall, it is a city of tall people. If he is short the streets are full of dwarfs; if ugly, ten perfect horrors pass him in one block; if beautiful, the competition is overwhelming. If he is talented, talent is a dime a dozen. If he tries to make an impression by wearing a toga—there's a man down the street in a leopard skin. Whatever he does or says or wears or thinks he is not unique. Once accepted this gives him perfect freedom to be himself, but unaccepted it horrifies him.

I don't think New York City is like other cities. It does not have character like Los Angeles or New Orleans. It is all characters—in fact, it is everything. It can destroy a man, but if his eyes are open it cannot bore him.

New York is an ugly city, a dirty city. Its climate is a scandal, its politics are used to frighten children, its traffic is madness, its competition is murderous. But there is one thing about it—once you have lived in New York and it has become your home, no place else is good enough.

FLAMMANTIA MOENIA DEMIMUNDI

Mark all these things: her generous reckless moods,
Proud, spendthrift, swift, assured, and terrible;
And make interpretation of your own.
But just one *caveat*:
She is not always merely what she seems:
I'd like to have you see her as I do—
The greatest unwrit poem in the world.

Christopher Morley
1945

The editors and publisher thank all those who so generously gave permission for the reproduction herein of texts and illustrations. Every possible effort has been made to obtain the proper permissions and to present the works in a manner satisfactory to the writers and artists. We encountered many fine writings about New York and regret that we could not include them all.

The Writers

11. Truman Capote. "The Diamond Iceberg." From *The Dog's Bark: Public People and Private Places*. Reprinted by permission of Random House. Copyright 1950 by Truman Capote. Washington Irving. "Golden Dreams." From *Tales of a Traveller*, 1824.

12. Mark Helprin. *A Winter's Tale*. Reprinted by permission of Harcourt Brace Jovanovich, Inc. Copyright 1983 by Mark Helprin.

13. Marie Ganz and Nat Ferber. *Rebels*. Reprinted by permission of Dodd, Mead and Co., Inc. Copyright 1920 by Dodd, Mead and Co., Inc.

14. Michael Gold. *Jews Without Money*. Copyright 1930, 1958, by Michael Gold.
O. Henry. "The Sparrows in Madison Square." From *Waifs and Strays*, 1917. Reprinted by permission of Doubleday & Co. Copyright 1904 by the *World*.

16. Piri Thomas. *Down These Mean Streets*. Reprinted by permission of Random House. Copyright 1967 by Piri Thomas.
James Baldwin. *Go Tell It on the Mountain*. Reprinted by permission of Doubleday & Co. Copyright 1952, 1953, by James Baldwin.
Thomas Eaton. "Descriptive View of New York." From *Review of New York*, 1814.

17. Langston Hughes. "Stars." Reprinted by permission of Random House, Inc. Copyright 1947 by Langston Hughes.

19. Anonymous. *Sunshine and Shadow*. Harper & Row. Reprinted by permission of Roger Whitehouse. Copyright 1974 by Roger Whitehouse.
Thomas Wolfe. "Enchanted City." From *The Web and the Rock*. Reprinted by permission of Harper & Row, Inc. Copyright 1937, 1938, 1939, by Maxwell Perkins, Executor; renewed 1965 by Paul Gitlin, Administrator of the Estate of Thomas Wolfe.
Damon Runyon, Jr. "Damon Runyon's Ashes." From *Father's Footsteps*. Reprinted by permission of Random House. Copyright 1953 by Damon Runyon, Jr.

20. O. Henry. "The Making of a New Yorker." From *The Trimmed Lamp*, 1907.

21. John Lennon. "Lennon Remembers." From *Rolling Stone* interview. Reprinted by permission of Straight Arrow Press. Copyright 1971.

22. Charles Dickens. *American Notes*, 1842.
Adriaen Van der Donck. "Of the Fishes." From *A Description of the New Netherlands*, 1653.

24. Washington Irving. *Knickerbocker's History of New York*, 1809.
Daniel Denton. *A Brief Description of New York, Formerly Called New Netherlands*, 1670.

26. Michael Gold. *Jews Without Money*. Copyright 1930, 1958, by Michael Gold.

27. Walt Whitman. "Give Me the Splendid Silent Sun." From *Leaves of Grass*, 4th ed., 1867.
Paul Morand. *New York*. Reprinted by permission of Flammarion, Paris. Copyright 1930 by Flammarion.
Ogden Nash. "City Greenery." Reprinted by permission of Curtis Brown Ltd. Copyright 1947 by Ogden Nash.
Edward S. Martin. *The Wayfarer in New York*, 1909.

29. Edward Field. "Roaches." From *A Full Heart*. Reprinted by permission of Sheep Meadow Press. Copyright 1977 by Edward Field.

30. Herman Melville. *Moby-Dick*, 1851.
Joseph Mitchell. *Old Mr. Flood*, 1948. Reprinted by permission of Harold Ober Associates, Inc. Copyright 1944 by Joseph Mitchell. First appeared in *The New Yorker*.
Brander Matthews. *Outlines in Local Color*. Harper, 1898.

31. Thomas Wolfe. "Enchanted City." From *The Web and the Rock*. Reprinted by permission of Harper & Row, Inc. Copyright 1937, 1938, 1939, by Maxwell Perkins, Executor; renewed 1965 by Paul Gitlin, Administrator of the Estate of Thomas Wolfe.
Appleton's Dictionary of New York City. Appleton & Co., 1879.
Betty Smith. *A Tree Grows in Brooklyn*. Reprinted by permission of Harper & Row. Copyright 1943 by Betty Smith.

33. Joseph Mitchell. "The Rivermen." From *The Bottom of the Harbor*. Little, Brown Co., 1959. Reprinted by permission of Harold Ober Associates, Inc. Copyright 1959 by Joseph Mitchell. First appeared in *The New Yorker*.
Michael Gold. *Jews Without Money*. Copyright 1930, 1958, by Michael Gold.
Adriaen Van der Donck. "Of the Air." From *A Description of the New Netherlands*, 1653.
Philip Hone. *Diary of Philip Hone*, 1835.

34. James Kirke Paulding. "The Narrows and New York Bay." From *New Mirror for Travellers; and Guide to the Springs*, 1828.
Thomas De Voe. *The Market Assistant*, 1867.
Meyer Berger. *Meyer Berger's New York*. Reprinted by permission of Random House, Inc. Copyright 1953–60 by Mae G. Berger, Executrix of the Estate of Meyer Berger.

36. Thomas Wolfe. "Enchanted City." From *The Web and the Rock*. Reprinted by permission of Harper & Row, Inc. Copyright 1937, 1938, 1939, by Maxwell Perkins, Executor; renewed

1965 by Paul Gitlin, Administrator of the Estate of Thomas Wolfe.
Joe Madden. "And Now, Good Night." From *Who the Hell Cares?* Published by Madden, 1948.

40. James Fenimore Cooper. *Home as Found*, 1832.
Felix Riesenberg, *East Side, West Side*, 1927. Reprinted by permission of Felix Riesenberg, III.

41. H. C. Bunner. *The Story of a New York House*, 1887.

42. W. Parker Chase. "New York in 1982 à la Bellamy." From *New York, the Wonder City*, 1932. Reprinted by New York Bound, 1983.
Gilbert Millstein. *God and Harvey Grosbeck*. Reprinted by permission of Doubleday & Co. Copyright 1983 by Gilbert Millstein.

44. Calvin Trillin. *Floater*. Reprinted by permission of Ticknor & Fields. Copyright 1980 by Calvin Trillin, Alice Trillin and Arthur B. Kramer as Trustee u/t/a.
Appleton's Dictionary of New York City. Appleton & Co., 1887.
Ernest Poole. *The Harbor*. Reprinted by permission of Macmillan Publishing Co. Copyright 1915, 1943, by Ernest Poole.

45. Jack Finney. *Time and Again*. Reprinted by permission of Simon & Schuster. Copyright 1970 by Jack Finney.
Philip Hone. *Diary of Philip Hone*, 1835.

46. Gay Talese. *The Bridge*. Reprinted by permission of Harper & Row, Inc. Copyright 1964 by Gay Talese.
Charles Hanson Towne. "New Buildings," 1908.

47. Louis Auchincloss. "The Landmarker." From *Tales of Manhattan*. Reprinted by permission of Houghton Mifflin, Co. Copyright 1964, 1966, 1967, by Louis Auchincloss.
William Archer. *America Today*, 1899.

48. Theodore Dreiser. *The Color of a Great City*. Reprinted by permission of Harold J. Dies, The Dreiser Trust. Copyright 1923 by Boni & Liveright.
Stephen Graham. *New York Nights*. Reprinted by permission of Doubleday & Co. Copyright 1927 by G. H. Doran Co.
F. Scott Fitzgerald. "My Lost City," 1932. From *The Crack-Up*. Reprinted by permission of New Directions Publishing Corp. Copyright 1945 by New Directions.
Helen Keller. "A Romantic Edifice." Reprinted by permission of The American Foundation for the Blind.

51. Theodore Dreiser. *Sister Carrie*, 1900.
Mark Twain. "John Chinaman in New York," 1870.

52. William Riordan. "Tammany Leaders Not Bookworms." From *Plunkitt of Tammany Hall*. McClure Phillips, 1905.

53. Charles Dickens. *American Notes*, 1842.
John Sloan. *John Sloan's New York*. Reprinted by permission of Harper & Row, Inc.

Copyright 1965 by Helen Farr Sloan.

54. Stephen Crane. "A Detail." From *Midnight Sketches*, in *Pocket Magazine*, Vol. I, Oct. 1896.

55. Henry Roth. *Call It Sleep.* Reprinted by permission of Roslyn Targ Literary Agency, Inc. Copyright 1934 by Henry Roth; renewed 1962 by Henry Roth.

56. Benjamin De Casseres. *Mirrors of New York.* Published by Joseph Lawren, 1925. Copyright 1925 by Benjamin De Casseres.

57. Anonymous. *Prostitution Exposed: Or, a Moral Reform Dictionary,* 1839.

58. Don Freeman. "Apple Annie." From *Come One Come All.* Reprinted by permission of Holt, Rinehart and Winston. Copyright 1949 by Don Freeman.

60. Damon Runyon. "Cafe Society." From *My Wife Ethel.* Reprinted by permission of King Features Syndicate Division, The Hearst Corp. Copyright 1939 by King Features.

61. Upton Sinclair. *The Metropolis,* 1907.

62. Henry Miller. "The Ghetto." From *The Henry Miller Reader.* Reprinted by permission of New Directions Publishing Corp. Copyright 1959 by Henry Miller. Originally appeared in *Sexus,* 1949.
Theodore L. Kazimiroff. "A Strange Meeting." From *The Last Algonquin.* Reprinted by permission of Theodore L. Kazimiroff. Copyright 1982 by T. Kazimiroff.

64. Gene Schermerhorn. *Letters to Phil,* 1886. Reprinted by permission of New York Bound. Copyright 1982 by New York Bound.
Christopher Morley. "When You're Writing." From *A Mandarin in New York.* Reprinted by permission of Harper & Row, Inc. Copyright 1933 by Christopher Morley; renewed 1961 by Mrs. Helen F. Morley.

66. Guido Bruno. "Way Down in Greenwich Village." From *Adventures in American Bookshops, Antique Stores and Auction Rooms.* Copyright 1922 by Guido Bruno.
Red Smith. "The Sporting Life." From *New York Herald Tribune Presents New York New York.* Copyright 1964 by the New York Herald Tribune, Inc. Reprinted by permission of Mrs. Red Smith.
Edith Wharton. *The Age of Innocence.* Reprinted by permission of Charles Scribner's Sons. Copyright 1920 by Edith Wharton; renewed 1948 by William R. Tyler.

68. A. J. Liebling. "The Telephone Booth Indian," 1944. Reprinted by permission of Russell & Volkening, Inc. Copyright 1937, 1939–42 by A. J. Liebling; renewed 1965, 1967–70 by A. J. Liebling.

69. Henry Miller. "The Ghetto." From *The Henry Miller Reader.* Reprinted by permission of New Directions Publishing Corp. Copyright 1959 by Henry Miller. Originally appeared in *Sexus,* 1949.

70. Betty Smith. *A Tree Grows in Brooklyn.* Reprinted by permission of Harper & Row.

Copyright 1943 by Betty Smith.
Joe Madden. "White Horses en Route to Track." From *Who the Hell Cares?* Published by Madden, 1948.
Russell Baker. *The Night the Lights Went Out.* Reprinted by permission of The New York Times Company. Copyright 1965 by The New York Times Company.

72. Joseph Mitchell. *My Ears Are Bent.* Reprinted by permission of Harold Ober Associates, Inc. Copyright 1938 by Joseph Mitchell.

74. William Dean Howells. *A Hazard of New Fortunes,* 1890.

75. Cecil Beaton. *Cecil Beaton's New York.* London, 1938.
Mark Twain. "The Sex in New York." From *Mark Twain's Travels with Mr. Brown,* 1867. Reprinted by permission of Alfred A. Knopf, Inc.
Newman Levy and John Held, Jr. "Grand Central Station." From *Saturday to Monday,* 1930. Reprinted by permission of Mrs. Eva Levy Marshall.

77. Herman Melville. "First Night of Their Arrival in the City." From *Pierre,* 1852.

78. Christopher Morley. *Swiss Family Manhattan.* Reprinted by permission of Harper & Row, Inc. Copyright 1932 by Christopher Morley.

79. Helen Keller. *Midstream.* Reprinted by permission of The American Foundation for the Blind. Copyright 1929 by Helen Keller.

80. "The Fulton Ferry." From the *New York Mirror,* January 2, 1836.
Theodore Dreiser. *The Color of a Great City.* Reprinted by permission of Harold J. Dies, The Dreiser Trust. Copyright 1923 by Boni & Liveright.

81. Walt Whitman. "Broadway." From *Leaves of Grass,* 8th ed., 1888.
Joel H. Ross, M.D. *What I Saw in New-York,* 1851.

82–83. Edward Sorel. "The Rise and Fall of the Taxi," 1984. Originally published in *New York Magazine.* Copyright 1984 by Edward Sorel.

84. Isaac S. Lyon. *Recollections of an Old Cartman,* 1872; repr. 1983. Reprinted by permission of New York Bound.

85. Sean O'Casey. *Rose and Crown.* Reprinted by permission of Macmillan Publishing Co. Copyright 1952 by Sean O'Casey; renewed 1980 by Eileen O'Casey.
James Kirke Paulding. "A Southern Lady Delights in the City." From *New Mirror for Travellers; and Guide to the Springs,* 1828.
E. B. White. "Commuter." From *The Lady Is Cold,* 1946. Reprinted by permission of Harper & Row, Inc. Copyright 1925 by E. B. White. Originally appeared in *The New Yorker.*

86. Stephen Crane. "Transformed Boulevard" (New York's Bicycle Speedway). From the *New York Sun,* July 5, 1896.

87. Elizabeth Oates Smith. *A Jam in Broadway,* 1854.

88. Ogden Nash. "What Street Is This, Driver?" From *Good Intentions.* Reprinted by permission of Little, Brown & Co. Copyright 1942 by Ogden Nash.

89. James Dickey. "For the Running of the New York City Marathon." From *The Strength of Fields.* Reprinted by permission of Doubleday & Co. Copyright 1979 by James Dickey.

90. Piri Thomas. *Down These Mean Streets.* Reprinted by permission of Random House. Copyright 1967 by Piri Thomas.
Avery Corman. *The Old Neighborhood.* Reprinted by permission of Simon & Schuster. Copyright 1980 by Avery Corman.

93. Alfred Kazin. *A Walker in the City.* Reprinted by permission of Harcourt Brace Jovanovich, Inc. Copyright 1951 by Alfred Kazin.
Helen Keller. "I Go Adventuring." From *Midstream.* Reprinted by permission of The American Foundation for the Blind. Copyright 1929 by Heller Keller.

94. Mark Helprin. *A Winter's Tale.* Reprinted by permission of Harcourt Brace Jovanovich, Inc. Copyright 1983 by Mark Helprin.
F. Scott Fitzgerald. "My Lost City," 1932. From *The Crack-Up.* Reprinted by permission of New Directions Publishing Corp. Copyright 1945 by New Directions.
Delmore Schwartz. "America, America!" From *The Last and Lost Poems of Delmore Schwartz.* Reprinted by permission of The Vanguard Press. Copyright 1954 by Delmore Schwartz.

97. Bernard G. Richards. "My Vacation on the East Side." From *Discourses of Keidansky,* 1903. Reprinted by permission of Ruth Richards Eisenstein and the Estate of Bernard G. Richards.

98. Charles G. Shaw. *Night Life.* Published by John Day Co., 1931.

99. Henry David Thoreau. "Letter to R. W. Emerson." From *The Writings of Henry David Thoreau. Familiar Letters, Years of Discipline,* 1843.
E. B. White. "Village Revisited." From *Poems and Sketches of E. B. White.* Reprinted by permission of Harper & Row, Inc. Copyright 1944 by E. B. White. Originally appeared in *The New Yorker.*

100. Michael Gold. *Jews Without Money.* Copyright 1930, 1958, by Michael Gold.
James Baldwin. *Go Tell It on the Mountain.* Reprinted by permission of Doubleday & Co. Copyright 1952, 1953, by James Baldwin.
Marianne Moore. "New York." From *Collected Poems.* Reprinted by permission of Macmillan Publishing Co. Copyright 1935 by Marianne Moore; renewed 1963 by Marianne Moore and T. S. Eliot.

101. Lewis Mumford. "New York Realists." From *My Work and Days.* Reprinted by permission of Harcourt Brace Jovanovich, Inc. Originally appeared in *The New Yorker,* 1937.

102. John Reed. "Forty-Two Washington Square." From *The Day in Bohemia,* 1913.

Joyce Kilmer. "Incongruous New York." From *The Circus and Other Essays.* Reprinted by permission of Doubleday & Co. Copyright 1916 by George Doran Co.

103. Kate Simon. "Battles and Celebrations." From *Bronx Primitive.* Reprinted by permission of Viking Penguin. Copyright 1982 by Kate Simon.

Harvey Shapiro. "Brooklyn Heights." From *The Light Holds.* Reprinted by permission of Wesleyan University Press. Copyright 1984 by Harvey Shapiro.

105. Edmund Wilson. *Memoirs of Hecate County.* Reprinted by permission of Farrar, Straus & Giroux, Inc. Copyright 1942 by Edmund Wilson.

F. Scott Fitzgerald. "My Lost City," 1932. From *The Crack-Up.* Reprinted by permission of New Directions Publishing Corp. Copyright 1945 by New Directions.

108. Thomas Wolfe. "Enchanted City." From *The Web and the Rock.* Reprinted by permission of Harper & Row, Inc. Copyright 1937, 1938, 1939, by Maxwell Perkins, Executor; renewed 1965 by Paul Gitlin, Administrator of the Estate of Thomas Wolfe.

Robert Benchley. *The Benchley Roundup.* Reprinted by permission of Harper & Row, Inc. Copyright 1928 by Harper & Row; renewed 1956 by Gertrude D. Benchley.

109. Christopher Morley. "Epitaph for Any New Yorker." From *Parson's Pleasure.* Reprinted by permission of Harper & Row. Copyright 1923 by Christopher Morley.

Floyd Dell. *Love in Greenwich Village.* George H. Doran, 1926.

110. Will Rogers. "New York's Five Boroughs Celebrate," 1923. From *A Will Rogers Treasury.* Reprinted by permission of Crown Publishers, Inc. Copyright 1982 by Bryan Sterling and Frances N. Sterling.

Christopher Morley. "Skyline." From *The New York World's Fair 1939 Prospectus.* Copyright 1936 by New York World's Fair Corporation 1939, Inc.

113. Sinclair Lewis. "That Was New York and That Was Me." Reprinted by permission of The New Yorker Magazine, Inc. Copyright 1937, 1965, by The New Yorker Magazine, Inc.

Theodore Dreiser. My City, 1929. Reprinted by permission of Harold J. Dies, The Dreiser Trust.

Mark Twain. *Mark Twain's Travels with Mr. Brown,* 1867. Reprinted by permission of Alfred A. Knopf, Inc.

116. Weegee. "Sunday Morning in Manhattan." From *Naked City.* Essential Books, 1945. Reprinted by permission of Wilma Wilcox, Curator, The Weegee Collection.

Edward Field. "New York." Reprinted by permission of Sheep Meadow Press. Copyright 1977 by Edward Field.

118. John Updike. "Central Park." From *Assorted Prose.* Reprinted by permission of Alfred A. Knopf, Inc. Copyright 1956 by John Updike.

119. Pete Hamill. *The Invisible City.* Reprinted by permission of Random House, Inc. Copyright 1980 by Pete Hamill.

120. Gregory Corso. From *New York True North.* Reprinted by permission of New Directions Publishing Corp. Copyright 1964 by Gregory Corso.

121. Allen Ginsberg. "Waking in New York. Part II." From *Collected Poems 1947–1980.* Reprinted by permission of Harper & Row, Inc. Copyright 1964, 1984, by Allen Ginsberg.

E. B. White. *Here Is New York.* Reprinted by permission of Harper & Row. Copyright 1949 by E. B. White.

122. Joseph Mitchell. *The Bottom of the Harbor.* Little, Brown Co., 1959. Reprinted by permission of Harold Ober Associates, Inc. Copyright 1959 by Joseph Mitchell. First appeared in *The New Yorker.*

John Steinbeck. *Autobiography: The Making of a New Yorker.* Reprinted by permission of The New York Times Company. Copyright 1953 by The New York Times Company.

123. Christopher Morley. "Flammantia Moenia Demimundi." Reprinted by permission of Harper & Row. Copyright 1945 by Christopher Morley.

The Artists

2–3. James E. Allen. *Builders.* Etching, 1937. Courtesy Mary Ryan Gallery, New York.

4. Vernon Howe Bailey. Pen and ink drawing from *The New York Times* (magazine), February 27, 1910. Private collection.

7. Anonymous. Woodcut from *Light and Shadow,* c. 1900.

8. Isac Friedlander. *Brooklyn Fog.* Etching, 1939. Courtesy Mary Ryan Gallery, New York.

10. Maxfield Parrish. Pen and ink drawing from *Knickerbocker's History of New York* by Washington Irving, 1898.

12. Thomas Nast. *New York in a Few Years from Now: View from the Bay.* Engraving from *Harper's Weekly,* 1882.

13. Harvey Dinnerstein. Charcoal drawing, 1973. Courtesy the artist. (Photograph by Geoffrey Clements)

15. Stanley Fox. *The Sparrows' Home, Union Square, New York City.* Engraving from *Harper's Weekly,* 1869.

17. Tom Sciacca. *Humpty Dumpty.* Mixed media, 1985. Courtesy the artist.

18. Louis Lozowick. *New York.* Lithograph, 1925. Courtesy Mary Ryan Gallery, New York.

19. Anonymous. Matchbook for the Stork Club. c. 1927. Courtesy New York Bound Bookshop.

20. Lou Beach. Collage, 1982. Courtesy the artist.

21. Eve Chwast. Woodcut, 1986. Courtesy the artist.

22. Anonymous. *Wild Animals of the New Netherlands.* Engraving, c. 1830.

23. Anonymous. *Central Park: The Ramble.* Engraving from *Harper's Weekly,* 1860. Courtesy Urban Graphics, New York.

24. Andrezj Dudzinski. Colored pencil drawing, 1979. Courtesy the artist.

25. Guy Billout. Watercolor and airbrush, from *Thunderbolt and Rainbow,* 1980. Courtesy the artist.

26. George Bellows. *In the Park Dark.* Lithograph, 1916. Courtesy Mary Ryan Gallery, New York.

27. Seymour Chwast. Pen and ink drawing, 1986. Courtesy the artist.

28. Robert Andrew Parker. *Gregor Samsa in America: New York Night II.* Etching and watercolor, 1979. Courtesy the artist.

29. Seymour Chwast. Pen and ink drawing, 1986. Courtesy the artist.

30. Seymour Chwast. Pen and ink drawing, 1986. Courtesy the artist.

32. Anonymous. *New York City—Building Contrasts.* Engraving from *Harper's Weekly,* 1889. Courtesy Urban Graphics, New York.

33. Anonymous. *First Settlement of New York.* Engraving from *Lights and Shadows of New York,* date unknown.

35. James Grashow. *House Plants.* Plywood, 1985. Courtesy the artist.

37. S. L. Margolies. *Man's Canyons.* Etching/aquatint, c. 1937. Courtesy Mary Ryan Gallery, New York.

38–39. Anonymous. Lithographs, c. 1880. Courtesy New York Bound Bookshop.

41. Tony Sarg. *The Flatiron Building.* Pen and ink drawing from *Tony Sarg's New York,* 1926.

42. Charles Sheeler. *Delmonico Building.* Lithograph, 1926. Courtesy Mary Ryan Gallery, New York.

43. R. O. Blechman. Pen and ink with watercolor, 1982. Courtesy the artist.

44. Anonymous. Engraving from *The Physiology of New York Boarding Houses,* 1857. Courtesy New York Bound Bookshop.

45. Seymour Chwast. Pen and ink drawing, 1986. Courtesy the artist.

46. Stow Wengenroth. *Manhattan Gateway.* Lithograph, 1948. Courtesy Mary Ryan Gallery, New York.

48. A. Maxwell Fry. *New York of the Future.* Pencil drawings from *Creative Art,* 1931.

49. Anonymous. *The Steel Globe Tower, 700 Feet High, Coney Island, New York.* Postcard, c. 1907.

50. W. S. L. Jewett. *Broadway, February 1868.* Engraving from *Harper's Weekly,* 1868.

51. C. Bunnell. *New York—A Game of Fan-Tan in a Gambling Den in Mott Street.* Engraving from *Once a Week,* 1891. Courtesy New York Bound Bookshop.

Index

The Writers

The Artists